W9-AGO-952

THE U. S. BORDER PATROL

Around the clock, every day of the year, inspectors of the United States Border Patrol guard America against illegal entry by aliens, smugglers and other persons not rightfully entitled to come here. Theirs is a challenging job and sometimes a dangerous one. Like the F.B.I., the Secret Service and the Forest Rangers, the bronzed, weather-beaten men of the Patrol are known and respected by citizens throughout the nation.

In **The U. S. Border Patrol** Clement David Hellyer provides an absorbing account of the colorful history, the rugged training and the unceasing vigilance of this important law enforcement agency.

THE U.S. BORDER PATROL

BY CLEMENT DAVID HELLYER

illustrated with U.S. Border Patrol photographs

Landmark
BOOKS

RANDOM HOUSE
NEW YORK

© Copyright, 1963, by Clement David Hellyer

All rights reserved under International and Pan-American
Copyright Conventions. Published in New York by
Random House, Inc., and simultaneously in Toronto, Canada, by
Random House of Canada, Limited. Manufactured in
The United States of America

Library of Congress catalog card number: 63-7803

FOR JOHN-BO

ACKNOWLEDGMENT

Without the coöperation of scores of Border Patrol Inspectors, both from the top echelons and from the rank-and-file, this account could never have been written. The author gratefully acknowledges his indebtedness to them all.

As the list is very long, only a few names can be included here. Of special help was Robert J. Seitz. James F. Greene, as Assistant Commissioner, Enforcement, Immigration and Naturalization Service, in direct charge of the Border Patrol, opened many doors which might otherwise have remained sealed.

Also acknowledged with sincere thanks is the contribution of Robin J. Clack, Paul K. Crosby, Edgar C. Niebuhr, William M. Davis, Walter R. Hayfield, Thomas L. Ball, George W. Harrison, Robert L. Jarratt, Edward A. Smith, Joseph C. White, William A. Turner, Chester W. Wilson, Marcus Neelly, Chester Woish, Merrill Toole, Armour E. Smith and Robert W. Brennan.

C.D.H.

CONTENTS

FOREWORD

The United States Border Patrol is one of the operating branches in the Immigration and Naturalization Service, a division of the Department of Justice. The Patrol has, as its principal responsibility, the duty of guarding the borders of the United States against the entry of persons not rightfully entitled to come here. In addition, it participates, with the other enforcement arms of the Service, in searching out and apprehending those who manage to enter in violation of law, so that their expulsion can be speedily accomplished.

In this book you will read about the progress and work of the Border Patrol since its origin some forty years ago; its present activities, and about some of the people with whom it is concerned. When you do so, keep in mind a picture of the map of the United States with its thousands of miles of land and sea borders, which offer such appealing attractions to the thousands, in fact millions, of people abroad who are unable to enter this country legally, and who hope to find through those vast borders an easy path into the United States. Resisting this threat to the internal welfare and security of the United States is one of the major functions of the Border Patrol.

I hope that this book will bring you an exciting and interesting experience and an insight into the workings of a United States law enforcement agency whch is so intensely concerned with the internal well-being of your country.

Raymond F. Farrell

Commissioner
Immigration and Naturalization Service
United States Department of Justice

THE U. S. BORDER PATROL

1
FIND 'EM, SEIZE 'EM, SEND 'EM HOME

Under a pale winter moon, the Arizona desert sleeps.

Close to the United States-Mexican border south of Yuma, Arizona, two pinpoints of light dance among the sand dunes. These tiny torches are the headlights of a jeep, which is picking its way gingerly through the sage and cactus.

Piloting the tough little vehicle is an inspector of the United States Border Patrol. He and a fellow officer, on routine duty, are combing the lonely wasteland for "border jumpers"—aliens, or foreigners, who have crossed the frontier on foot from Mexico.

They know that any noncitizen who enters our land in the dead of night, across such a forbidding desert, is a lawbreaker. Otherwise he would cross the line in daylight at any one of the many legal entry points. And he would carry with him the documents required for lawful entry into the United States.

Bouncing through the warm night, the Border Patrol Inspectors peer through the windshield, alert for "sign." To them, sign is any evidence that a border jumper has recently passed their way: footprints in the sand, a dislodged stone, candy wrappers, a cigarette butt, a branch freshly broken from a bush. Their trained eyes miss few clues.

This same winter's night, while the jeep team scouts the Mexican border, another pair of Border Patrol Inspectors is engaged in a dangerous mission far to the north. There, along the Canadian border in Minnesota, deep snow carpets the frozen earth.

Night air settles, damp and piercing, around two heavily clad figures huddled near the base of a giant pine. For hours, these two inspectors have sat quietly, waiting. They deny themselves the rude comfort of a fire, aware that the tiniest flame will betray their whereabouts to a band of smugglers they hope to surprise this night.

Meanwhile, far to the south and east in the tepid waters of the Gulf of Mexico, a powerful speedboat rams its way through the gloom. Aboard, still another team of Border Patrol Inspectors scans the moonlit horizon, alert for the profile of a certain vessel. Hours earlier, Patrol intelligence units received information that a boatload of aliens was heading for the Florida coast, hoping to land without the necessary entry documents.

At the same moment, at other points along the international frontiers of the United States, and in many major seaports, other Patrol Inspectors are scanning the faces of passengers pouring through bus and train terminals. More members of the Patrol are manning highway check points near international lines, and still more probe the interiors and under-sides of freight trains in a tireless, never-ending search for border jumpers.

Patrol Inspectors may be bouncing in a jeep over the warm desert sands of Arizona or kneeling beneath a pine in the freezing wilds of Minnesota. They may be piloting a speedboat in the Gulf or manning a highway check point in California. But wherever

FAR-FLUNG GUARDIANS OF THE U.S. BORDERS

A Patrol Inspector along the Gulf of Mexico points out possible hiding places aboard ship during a hunt for stowaways at Mobile City Docks.

In the rugged Sandhills Area west of El Paso, two inspectors follow the tracks of aliens under the hot Texas sun.

Far to the north, two Patrolmen drive their jeep through the deep snows that cover the North Dakota border sector.

they are their mission is the same: find 'em, seize
'em, send 'em home.

So it is, around the clock, every day of the year,
inspectors of the Border Patrol guard America against
invasion by those who have no legal business being
in the country. Theirs is a tough and important
assignment, and sometimes a dangerous one. It is no
puny task to keep constant vigil over the 8,000 miles
of border wasteland, forest, mountain, lake and sea
for which the Patrol is responsible.

These men in forest-green truly rate the title:
Guardians of our borders.

Today's United States Border Patrol is the uni-
formed enforcement division of the United States
Immigration and Naturalization Service (USINS).
The USINS is an agency within the Department of
Justice, and its top commander is the Commissioner
of Immigration and Naturalization. His chief su-
perior is the Attorney General of the United States.

A small army of trained experts—some 1,700 strong
—makes up today's Patrol. Most of these men are
Patrol Inspectors (or PIs, as they sometimes call
themselves). Officially, they are listed on the government payroll as Immigration Patrol Inspectors, but

this long-winded designation is rarely used outside of government literature.

Patrol Inspectors derive their authority from an Act of Congress which was enacted on February 27, 1925, and is now a part of the Immigration and Naturalization Act of June 27, 1952. They work directly for the United States government. Under this Act of Congress, PIs may, without a warrant, arrest any alien who, in their presence or view, enters or tries to enter the United States illegally.

They are also authorized to board and search for aliens, without warrant, any vessel within the territorial waters of the United States, or any train, airplane or other vehicle within a reasonable distance from any boundary of the nation.

Under United States laws, it is a crime to make false statements in an effort to enter the country, or to evade inspection by immigration officers, or to enter at a time or place not designated as a port of entry for aliens. So anyone who jumps the border is, under this definition, a criminal, no matter how innocent he may consider his reasons for entering.

United States law provides stiff penalties for illegal entries. For first offenses, the penalty is six months' imprisonment or a $500 fine, or both. For a second infraction, it increases. And if an alien has been formally deported, the law provides two years in jail, $1,000 in fines, or both, if he is caught jumping the line again.

For smugglers of aliens, the law has special contempt: the punishment is a $2,000 fine or five years in jail, or both, for *each* alien smuggled.

An alien may be sentenced to three years in prison for making a false claim to United States citizenship —as many do—or he may be fined $1,000, or both. Some buy forged documents for as much as $500, or steal genuine identification papers from United States citizens traveling abroad. In one recent case, United States officials found four different aliens, in four different states, using identical birth certificates to "prove" their United States citizenship.

Finding and arresting such violators is the mission of the Border Patrol. It is challenging work, and it can be dangerous. Between 1919 and 1960, fifty-two officers lost their lives in the line of duty. Many were struck down brutally by the guns or knives of aliens they were tracking or arresting. Others were mercilessly mangled by cars driven by vicious lawbreakers, who smashed through highway check points with cargoes of smuggled aliens or contraband.

The PI's job calls for quick decisions and cool thinking. Officers who fail to keep their heads in emergencies may pay for their mistakes with their lives. This happened to one young officer in El Paso, Texas.

The young PI had just arrested an alien on a downtown street. He searched his man—a procedure followed faithfully by every inspector—and found a wickedly sharp boning knife. The officer confiscated the weapon and loaded his prisoner into the back seat of his patrol car. The PI then climbed into the front seat behind the wheel. Carelessly, he laid the razor-sharp knife beside him on the front seat.

As the inspector paused a moment to light a cigarette, the prisoner suddenly reached over the back of the seat, grabbed the knife, and plunged it repeatedly into the PI's body. The first thrust was enough: it found his heart. The youthful inspector paid for a moment's thoughtlessness with his life.

His vicious killer was later declared insane and committed to an asylum.

2
MEET PEDRO, THE BORDER JUMPER

Though the Border Patrol is charged with protecting all boundaries of the United States from alien invasions, most of its activities are concentrated along the 2,013-mile frontier separating the United States from the republic of Mexico.

A certain amount of illegal entry occurs along the United States-Canadian border, and some unlawful landings are made in southern states bordering the Gulf of Mexico. Some seaports, too, are favored by aliens seeking illegal entry. But border-jumping traffic along the Mexican border far exceeds the traffic from all other sectors combined.

Most of those attempting to jump the Mexican-United States line are, of course, Mexican citizens. An occasional violator may be a citizen of some other land. He may be from another Latin American nation to the south of Mexico, or from islands in the Caribbean. Or he may be of European or Oriental extraction. Whoever he (or she) is, the alien cannot, or will not, for one reason or another, obtain the documents required for legal entry.

A few of these men and women are hardened criminals, and their motives in crossing the line are openly criminal. Because of this small percentage of seasoned criminals, the Border Patrol must always be on the alert for danger. But at the same time, the Patrol Inspectors realize that most of the border jumpers are not criminals. The majority of PIs like the Mexican people and feel a real sympathy for the hardships which drive so many of them to attempt to enter the country illegally.

Among PIs, the Mexican alien who jumps the line is known as a "wet," which is short for "wetback." The term originates from the fact that some Mexicans, to gain entry, swim or wade across the Rio

Grande to the Texas side. Those who choose this method of entry usually get their backs wet, hence the name "wetbacks." The label is now applied generally to all Mexicans who enter illegally, wet or dry.

Many would-be invaders, incidentally, die in their attempt to cross the Rio Grande. Now and then PIs find a body washed ashore. Those who succeed sometimes make the crossing on crude rafts or planks. Others have been known to inflate paper sacks, which they use as "water-wings" for the crossing.

The average Mexican alien—let us call him Pedro —is a quiet, shy fellow. Usually he hails from some small interior village with a strange-sounding name. More than likely he is a field worker.

Sometimes Pedro is merely searching for adventure when he swims the Rio Grande or steals silently across the line at some desert point. But more likely he is looking for work. He is hungry, and his family back home is hungry, too. Perhaps it was a poor season and his crops failed. Or maybe there are just not enough jobs to go around in his village. So Pedro heads north to the land of Tio Sam (Uncle Sam) where, his countrymen assure him, jobs are plentiful and the pay is good. He knows that some of his friends or acquaintances have earned enough in a year or so to buy themselves a farm back home. This is something most rural-dwelling Mexicans could not achieve in a lifetime of work at local rates. Frequently their home-town pay gives them just enough to buy food.

The wiser ones apply for and get documents which are issued under a United States-Mexican treaty and entitle them to work legally as farm hands in the United States. For many years these documented aliens have made an important contribution to United States agriculture, and during World War II this contribution helped feed the United States while its men went off to war.

Some Mexicans, however, cannot—or do not understand they must—get documents. So they jump the line. These are the aliens the Border Patrol must find, arrest and deport. Most illegal aliens, like most of their documented countrymen, are docile and friendly people. And most also are courteous, and hard workers.

PIs who have tracked a Mexican alien through desert and mountain have a healthy respect for the endurance and strength of these tough, wiry people. "Some of them can travel across open country at a speed of four miles an hour, keeping up this speed for ten or more hours at a stretch," one inspector recalled from experience. "They can do this almost without food. I have seen them striding along through the desert, reaching out to pluck a handful of mesquite beans, eating them without breaking their stride."

This same inspector recalled one assignment in which he trailed a youngster who covered seventy miles in a little over twenty-four hours, on foot.

Mexicans who jump the line are, for the most part, a happy and carefree people. Most of them, when arrested, accept their fate gracefully. They know they will be treated fairly, and that a hot meal and a bed await them at a USINS detention facility.

One youngster, captured near Yuma, crawled up on the back of the Patrol jeep and sat there quietly as the driver made his way back to base through the desert. After a few minutes, the Mexican asked:

"May I sing?"

Permission was granted, and the captured alien entertained the driver and his PI companion all the way home with Mexican folk songs sung at the top of his lungs.

Most inspectors like Pedro. They speak his language, they know his customs, and they understand his problems. Apprehended Mexicans usually are amazed at the good treatment they receive from the Border Patrol. They are especially grateful for the PI's honesty. All the alien's possessions are inventoried when he is booked at Patrol stations, and all his things are returned to him when he is sent home. Meantime he is housed and fed in a detention facility, which is *not* a jail. The beds are clean, and the food may be the best—and the first—he has had in some time.

There is a great deal of poetry in their souls. One, when arrested, was carrying a small chinaberry tree, a bundle of corn husks for wrapping tamales, and two rose bushes. These, he explained to the PIs, were the coin with which he hoped to buy food and housing as he went along. They were his only worldly possessions.

As a rule, PIs are compassionate in their treatment of captured aliens. In many cases they have saved the lives of captives found near starvation or suffering from illness or accident.

Patrol Inspectors once traced a suspect to a doctor's office in an isolated village. He had fallen, they found, beneath a freight train, and one of his legs

had been severed. With the doctor's approval, the
PIs rigged a comfortable bed in their Patrol car and
hurried the alien more than 100 miles to the nearest
hospital. En route, they treated him for shock.

They were credited with saving the alien's life.

3
"SEND TWO COFFINS..."

Oddly enough, it was a wave of illegal entries by Chinese, not Mexicans, which forced the formation of America's first Border Patrol.

Late in the 1800s, the United States government grew seriously alarmed over the heavy flow of Chinese laborers into the country. These laborers, accustomed to hard work, long hours and low pay, were giving ruinous competition to American workers. So the federal government passed the Chinese Exclusion Act, prohibiting the Orientals' entry into the nation.

This resulted in a thriving traffic in the smuggling of Chinese aliens across our land borders and through our seaports. At that time, the United States-Mexican frontier was entirely open—a sieve 2,013 miles long. There were a few scattered entry gates, but between them stretched hundreds of miles of desert, mountain and river, wide open to all who wished to cross them.

As the smuggling traffic in Chinese laborers grew to alarming proportions, the government decided it was time to act. Thus was appointed the forerunner of all Border Patrol Inspectors, the first immigration officer, whose mission was to halt and arrest smugglers and border jumpers.

His name was Jefferson Davis Milton. Even in those days, Jeff Milton was known throughout the great Southwest for his many feats of derring-do. Since then his fame has continued to grow until today he is almost a legendary figure.

Before he was given his badge as an immigration officer in 1904, Jeff Milton already had racked up quite a reputation as a Texas Ranger, deputy sheriff, customs inspector, chief of police, and Wells Fargo messenger. Once, while guarding a $10,000 payroll shipment for Wells Fargo, Jeff tangled with a gang of train robbers. He was badly wounded in the resulting exchange of bullets, but he shot and killed a notorious bandit named Three-Finger Jack. Later, as police chief of El Paso, Texas—a rough-and-ready frontier town in those times—Jeff cleaned out all the gamblers.

So when the time came for the federal government to appoint its first special officer to police the frontier, Jeff Milton was the logical choice. With his appointment in 1904, the foundations of the present fast-moving Border Patrol were laid.

While bouncing through the desert in their jeeps or relaxing after work, today's PIs like to swap yarns about pioneers of the patrol. Inevitably, Jeff Milton's name enters the discussion. There, all are agreed, was a real *hombre*.

Take that time, for example, when Jeff was ordered to track down three bank robbers who had jumped the line. He threw some grub into his saddlebag, checked his stock of ammunition, mounted up and rode off across the burning sands.

For several days nobody heard from Jeff. This was nothing to be concerned about. After all, Jeff had often been off in the sagebrush by himself for as long as three months at a stretch. Eventually, however, some of his friends began to worry. After all, the three bank robbers were known to be desperate men; if they had a chance they would kill Jeff as quickly as they would shoot a rattlesnake.

Just as Jeff's comrades began to organize a searching party, a telegram arrived. Its message, terse and concise, was to become immortal. It said, simply:

"Send two coffins and a doctor." Signed: Jeff Milton.

Naturally the coffins were not for Jeff. Neither was the doctor.

Jeff Milton was the first of a hardy band of border law-enforcement officers called, at the beginning, the Mounted Inspectors. The group's primary mission was apprehension of Chinese border jumpers, and of smugglers who helped the Chinese make the illegal crossing.

They had an additional assignment. Along the wide-open border, a plague of major robberies and petty thefts had broken out. The marauders would dash across the line from Mexico for a lightning haul, then dodge back into the sanctuary of Mexico with their loot. Jeff and his fellow officers were ordered to halt these raids and stem the Chinese traffic.

Little if any effort was made, however, to stop the

entry of Mexican citizens illegally into the country. This traffic was not recognized as a serious problem until nearly twenty years later. It did not achieve alarming proportions until World War II.

Soon after Jeff Milton and his hard-riding colleagues began their patrols, the name of the group was changed to Mounted Watchmen. This finally was altered to Mounted Guard, and under this title Jeff's group was to carry on until 1924. The Mounted Guard never numbered more than seventy-five men.

By 1924, tighter and tighter restrictions on entry of aliens into the United States had made the smuggling of aliens a profitable business. It became apparent to Washington officials that greater vigilance was needed. A bigger, better-organized border force had to be created.

So in 1924 Congress created the United States Border Patrol. Its official mission: "To detect and prevent the smuggling and unlawful entry of aliens across the land boundaries."

Until then, Border Patrol activities had centered principally on the Mexican border. In 1925 their scope was broadened to include vigilance over the Gulf Coast and Florida.

Before 1940 the Patrol was a wing of the Depart-

ment of Labor. Then it passed under jurisdiction
of the Department of Justice, where it has remained
ever since.

Today's fast-rolling Patrol, with an authorized force
of some 1,700 men, is a far cry from those long-gone
days when 75 horse-mounted officers were held responsible for 2,013 miles of frontier.

Marcus Neelly, one of many officers who rose from
the Patrol to a high-ranking post in the Immigration
Service, was reminiscing. "When I was in the Patrol,"
he said, "we patrolled on horseback. Today we can
put out one light aircraft and three jeeps, manned
by seven officers, and patrol more ground than we
could have covered with a hundred men on horseback.

"Of course," he added wryly, "in the El Paso dis-
trict they didn't have a hundred men. There were
only *two*."

The Mounted Guard's primary target was smuggling, principally the traffic in Chinese and liquor.
They weren't much concerned, at that time, with the
illicit entry of Mexicans.

"Unless we saw six or more of them in a group,"
one old-timer recalled, "we didn't give them a second
thought."

One light aircraft and three jeeps can patrol more ground than was
formerly covered by a hundred men on horseback.

The Mounted Guards were true frontiersmen. They lived in the open, without any official headquarters, and moved about as emergencies dictated. Many a bloody battle was fought between these hardy horsemen and the smugglers.

Some of the fiercest gun battles were with liquor contrabandists in the days of Prohibition. In 1917 Congress provided for an amendment to the Constitution which would make it unlawful to manufacture, sell or transport alcoholic beverages within the United States. It went into effect in 1920.

Operating in sparsely settled areas, smugglers would haul their liquor across the border in five-gallon cans, loading pack trains of horses with the contraband. The tins were filled with raw alcohol of very high grade. The smugglers, who received large sums of money for their illegal merchandise, were armed to resist arrest and quick to shoot. At least five Mounted Guardsmen died in the blaze of smugglers' six-shooters.

Smugglers alternated between liquor and Chinese aliens. One favorite trick was to sneak a group of Chinese into a populated area under cover of darkness, then load them into empty boxcars on a railroad siding. The smugglers would stack hay around the door of the boxcar to create the impression that it was loaded with hay. Then they would label the car with an address in some inland point, and vanish.

One guard, called by his fellow officers "the laziest man in the Pecos," grew tired of checking boxcars filled with hay. So he came up with an ingenious labor-saving device. One of his old comrades remembers it this way:

"He just couldn't see the point of running through all those cars. So he rigged himself up a gun that would shoot sneezing powder into all of them. He'd walk down a string of boxcars, giving each car a shot. Then he'd walk back along the string, listening for sneezes. He caught more Chinese than anyone in the territory!"

In one car alone, sixty Chinese were found. Their total food supply: one large pot of rice.

Among the pioneer officers most hated and feared by the smugglers was Curtis D. Mosley. The smugglers knew "Mose" well, and repeatedly tried to get him in a spot where they could kill him.

George Harrison, an inspector who worked with Mosley in the early days, recalls:

"One time in El Paso, Mose was attacked by three men at a four-way intersection. One smuggler closed

in on his left, another on his right, and the third one
directly in front of him. All three tried to shoot
Mose.

"But Mose was too fast for 'em. He killed all three
with his .351 Winchester. The coroner could only
find two dead smugglers, but Mose insisted there'd
been three and that he'd shot 'em all.

"Well, there'd been heavy rains, and the dirt roads
at the intersection were pitted with potholes filled
with muddy water. Sure enough, a day or two later
the third dead smuggler floated to the surface of one
of these mudholes!"

In another scrape with death, Mose pulled his
Model T Ford alongside a car containing three aliens.
The Mexicans, who turned out to be smugglers, instantly pulled their guns, and shot and killed two
companions riding in the Ford with Mosley. Mose
purposely fell from the driver's seat onto the road.
Then, as the Mexicans made a U-turn and stepped
on the gas, Mosley shot thirty times. Officers later
counted twenty-seven bullet holes in the Mexicans'
car.

One smuggler was killed outright. A second was
so badly wounded he died later, while the third—
also seriously injured—lived to be tried and sent to

the penitentiary.

Mosley, like many of his fellow officers, carried on in the fine tradition established by Jeff Milton. But Milton stood—and still stands—in a class by himself. Although he would shoot without a moment's hesitation in a crisis, he was compassionate and exceptionally kind to animals. He would not kill even a rattlesnake unless one threatened his life. Several times the deadly serpents crawled into Jeff's warm bedroll on the desert sand. Jeff, in appreciation for their consideration in not biting him, would merely shake them out of his bed and go back to sleep.

Several lawbreakers tried to ambush Jeff. One who tried got four bullets in the head and neck before he hit the ground. Meeting death face to face was no novelty to Jeff. Once in El Paso he was saved only by his badge. The tiny piece of metal deflected the deadly thrust of a would-be assassin's knife.

Too tough for bullets or knife blades, Jeff eventually died quietly in bed, of natural causes, at the age of eighty-five. He died in Tombstone, Arizona, near the Huachaca mountain country which he loved.

Today Jeff and the Mounted Guard are gone. But the traditions they set are revered and followed by the men of the modern Border Patrol.

4
OPERATION WETBACK

The years between 1924 and the end of World War
II were years of routine growth for the Border
Patrol. With the end of the war, however, the Patrol
faced the greatest challenge in its history: Operation
Wetback.

During the 1940s, while war blazed in Europe and
the Far East, millions of American workers had put
down their tools and left for the battlefields. Their
departure created serious gaps in the factories and
fields of America.

To fill these voids, especially in agriculture, thousands of Mexicans began to pour across the southern frontier to seek employment. The Border Patrol at that time was not equipped to control such a flood of illegal entries. At times their task appeared hopeless; for every alien they deported, five or ten poured in.

Throughout the war years and for some time after the end of the war with Japan, the north-bound tide continued. The Border Patrol did its best to contain the deluge. But this was not good enough.

By the spring of 1954, it became obvious to Washington officials that America was being overrun by illegal aliens.

"We had an outlaw society abroad in the land," one official commented. "A million aliens were living a hunted, illegal existence, right under our noses."

Where aliens were concentrated, crime rates rose drastically. In some United States institutions, as high as ninety per cent of the criminal inmates were illegal aliens.

Wages and working conditions for United States laborers were hurt by the competition of this army of illegal workers. The aliens would work for as little as ten cents an hour in some areas, often under the worst possible conditions. Certain unscrupulous American farmers took advantage of the aliens, threatening to expose them to the Border Patrol unless they worked for substandard wages.

This invasion of wetbacks was one of the first problems tackled by the administration of President Dwight D. Eisenhower. The problem was so serious that Attorney General Herbert Brownell, in 1953, laid plans to deploy Army troops along the border to halt the flood.

This plan, fortunately, was never put into effect. Instead, General Joseph Swing, former commander of the Sixth Army, took a first-hand look at the border, acting on orders from the President. Swing's inspection tour was secret. So was the fact that, a few weeks later, he was to be named Commissioner of Immigration and Naturalization by President Eisenhower.

General Swing was no stranger to the United States-Mexican frontier. As a young artillery officer, he had lived and worked along the border. He knew its terrain, and its problems.

Now he was to stem the tide of illegal immigrants. In effect, his orders were to seal the border.

By June of 1954, the General was ready. A massive

mop-up operation was to be launched, and the border was to be sealed. The newspapers quickly dubbed General Swing's plan "Operation Wetback."

The new commissioner assembled a special force of some 800 officers in southern California. These were organized into two task forces, which in turn were split into operational units of twelve men, each commanded by a senior officer. Every unit was self-contained, equipped to operate independently while maintaining contact with task force headquarters and patrol aircraft.

Some old-timers along the border viewed the operation with open skepticism.

"It won't work," they predicted, scornfully. "You can ship 'em home to Mexico, but they'll come right back. They always have."

Operation Wetback proved the forecasters wrong. Control of the border in the western sectors was achieved within a few weeks. Then, leaving behind sufficient strength to hold the line, the task forces moved into south Texas in mid-July. There again the operation scored victory.

In the course of a year, Operation Wetback brought about the arrest and deportation of more than a *million* aliens. In one week alone, in southern

California and western Arizona, inspectors apprehended 10,917 aliens. Uncounted thousands, knowing their time would soon come, left the United States to flee back to Mexico voluntarily.

In the heavily industrialized areas around Spokane, Chicago, Kansas City, St. Louis and Gary, some 20,000 aliens were found working in industrial jobs. They were deported. A few escaped detection. Wherever there was room to hide, they hid. In the central valley of California, a busy agricultural region with a special attraction for alien farm workers, inspectors found on one farm a series of underground tunnels, complete with trap doors. Aliens lived in these tunnels.

They were found in woodpiles and haylofts, in caves and basements. Some were well housed, but thousands lived an animal existence.

Night and day the drive moved relentlessly forward. By bus, rail, plane and boat, the aliens were hauled deep into their native Mexico, nearer their homes and farther from the temptation to return.

At the same time, the United States government launched a successful campaign to convince American farmers of the wisdom of hiring only legal, documented alien workers. Most farmers coöperated in

At Patrol headquarters an Assistant Commissioner and pilot plan a patrol flight over a busy farm area.

this program, and their backing played an important role in helping the Border Patrol to seal the line.

By 1955, arrests had dropped from a million in one year to about 220,000. This slumped to under 100,000 the following year, and was again cut in half in 1957. For the first time in a decade, the United States-Mexican frontier was secured. An official was able to say:

"The day of the impoverished, hungry farm worker entering to find a job illegally is, for all practical purposes, over. What we are now encountering is the repeating violator of immigration laws, and the hard-core element of criminals."

Before Operation Wetback, the Patrol's job had been nearly hopeless. But now the Border Patrol was transformed from a group of small, stationary, loosely organized units into a coördinated, flexible striking force subject to immediate movement to any part of the United States.

Today's Border Patrol is on instant call. Certain units are maintained on continual alert, ready to respond within twelve hours. Other units, acting as a backstop, are on seventy-two-hour call. Each unit includes twelve men. This high degree of flexibility makes for a lot of travel. Nowadays Border Patrol

Inspectors, collectively, cover more than 10,000,000 miles each year by plane, boat, car, horseback and on foot.

Though the trusty horse still is used on occasion in mountainous country where even a jeep cannot penetrate, the jeep and patrol car have for the most part replaced their four-footed predecessor of Mounted Guard days.

One inspector, remembering fondly the old days of the Guard, recalled the times his alert horse had warned him of the approach of danger.

"I guess automobiles are handy," he admitted. "But they can't prick up their ears!"

5
THE PATROL GETS ITS WINGS

Aircraft today play an indispensable role in the operations of the alert Border Patrol. At least two planes are on continual duty in every Patrol sector on the United States-Mexican frontier. Others perform valuable service along the Canadian border, while more fly air reconnaissance missions out of New Orleans and ports in Florida and central California.

To see at first-hand how a Patrol aircraft is employed, I visited Border Patrol headquarters at El

Paso. There I was turned over to Patrol Pilot Bill Turner.

Soon we were skimming over the rolling, scrub-dotted desert north of El Paso, barely a hundred feet above the sands. Turner could make his tiny, two-passenger craft do everything except fly sideways. One moment we would bank sharply to the left; the next instant we would be standing on our right wingtip as Inspector Turner checked the ground below for sign.

Suddenly Turner leveled off and pointed downward. Looking below, I saw a tiny figure in a straw hat running toward a clump of bushes.

A mile or so behind us, a Border Patrol jeep with two inspectors aboard was jouncing over the rock-strewn terrain. Turner picked up his air-to-ground intercom microphone and said:

"Got a live one here, directly under me."

Then, noting that the area was too rough for a jeep to move with any speed, he switched on his plane's public-address system. This useful rig allows the pilot to give orders to anyone on the ground through a powerful loud-speaker mounted flush with the plane's outer skin.

Banking sharply and heading back toward the

running figure in the sombrero, PI Turner spoke into the mike in Spanish:

"This is the Border Patrol. Turn around and walk out to the road."

Instantly the figure left the shadow of the bush where he had been hiding and headed toward the road, a mile or so to the rear. There, a short while later, the alien was picked up by the jeep team and hauled back to base for interrogation and deportation.

This alien was one of hundreds tracked down and apprehended every year by Border Patrol pilots working with jeep teams on the ground.

Aircraft first joined the Patrol in 1946. It was not until 1954, however, that air reconnaissance began to assume a major role in the Patrol's operations. Since then the air arm has been expanded, and the number of planes and pilots has been steadily increased.

By 1960 the Patrol had an authorized force of forty-seven pilots, and plans called for further expansion. Seven of these pilots were certified as commanders on multi-engined aircraft.

In addition to nearly fifty small craft used for observation flights, the Patrol flies a DC-4, two C-46s and three C-47s. The multi-engined aircraft are used to return to their homelands aliens who have been apprehended in the United States. The DC-4, specially outfitted as a hospital plane, makes periodic flights to faraway countries—mostly to European nations—to repatriate aliens who are physically or mentally disabled and have become expensive public-welfare cases in the United States.

Border Patrol pilots are fliers second, and Patrol Inspectors first.

"We think of pilots not as pilots, but as enforcement officers in airplanes," explained Joe White, while he was Assistant Chief of the Patrol in charge of air operations. "The airplane is merely a means of getting him where he can do his job—a jeep with wings. His primary mission is exactly the same as that of the man in the jeep or patrol car, on horseback or on foot—the detection and apprehension of aliens who have crossed our borders illegally."

Most PI pilots now in the service knew how to fly when they entered the Patrol. Most are former military fliers. Even with hundreds of hours of flight-time experience, however, all first became trainees and served their year of probationary duty like every other rookie Patrol officer. And they put in two years with the Patrol on the ground before

AIRCRAFT JOIN THE BORDER PATROL

The pilot of a Border Patrol plane follows tracks of aliens who have illegally crossed the International Boundary.

The information is radioed to a jeep patrolling in the area.

A Patrol Inspector closes in on the aliens' hiding place.

becoming eligible for the Border Patrol wings.

In addition to serving his probationary time on the ground, the candidate for wings must have at least 600 hours of flight time and must have an FAA commercial license before he can fly Patrol aircraft. Officers who did not come into the Patrol with a flight background also may become Inspector Pilots by studying on the side for their wings. The incentive is great, for the pay scale for Patrol Pilots is higher than for their fellow officers on the ground.

Most of the thousands of hours flown every year by PI pilots are uneventful and routine. Frequently, however, the airmen are called upon to exercise rare courage and judgment.

A pilot in the Big Bend area of Texas once spotted two aliens who, he suspected, had entered the country illegally. They were trudging through rough countryside where landing the small plane would prove difficult and hazardous. Nevertheless the PI managed to put down his Cub on the hard sand of a dry riverbed and take the aliens into custody. As his plane was a two-seater machine, he then faced the knotty problem of getting both his charges back to headquarters. If he left one behind while he flew the other back to base, the "abandoned" alien without doubt would head for the hills.

The pilot solved the riddle shrewdly. The country-side was so rocky that a barefoot man could move across it only with great care and not a little pain. So he ordered the man whom he was leaving behind to remove his shoes. He then loaded the first alien, plus the second man's shoes, aboard his plane and returned to base with Captive No. 1. On returning, he found the second alien, barefooted and resigned to his fate, sitting patiently on a rock awaiting his captor.

This riverbed landing was no rarity. Border Patrol pilots put their trusty craft down on the oddest of makeshift airports—cow pastures (first shooing away the cows with a pass or two over them), dirt roads, dry lake beds. Now and then they must shoo off a deer before landing.

Occasionally they may drag a wingtip or whack a fence post on one of these impromptu landings. But their general record is one of remarkable safety.

Pilots flying along the southern border are able to cut sign from the air. But heavy forest growth along much of the United States-Canadian frontier makes aerial sign cutting there next to impossible. Instead,

Patrol aircraft are used on the northern line to spot locations of American logging camps in which Canadian aliens may be working illegally. During the winter, when rivers freeze over, PI pilots fly the line to watch for tracks across the ice, or to spot the formation of ice bridges which might serve as paths for illegal entries.

One Patrol plane, operating from Grand Forks, North Dakota, is specially equipped for work in the area. A De Haviland four-seater, it carries pontoons and wheel gear for warm-weather operations, and converts to skis for winter landings on ice and snow.

Because of aircraft, fewer ground personnel are needed in large-scale mop-up operations in agricultural areas. In the cotton fields near McAllen, Texas, during the harvest season, one plane may team up with several patrol cars. Each car carries a giant number painted on its roof. The PI pilot flies over the cotton fields on reconnaissance. Then, spotting what he believes might be illegal aliens working below, he passes on this information by radio to his colleagues on the ground.

"Unit 2, I spot what might be a bunch of wets

(Above) Emergency survival gear carried in Beaver aircraft operating along the northern border. (Below) Border Patrol Inspector and pilot discuss plans for air-ground surveillance along the New York State border. Their aircraft is equipped with skis and wheels for landings on ice and snow.

at about four o'clock from your position, approximately a quarter of a mile from the fence."

Inspectors in Unit 2 then make a ground investigation of the workers. If the laborers have legal documents, they are permitted to continue; if not, they
are arrested and deported.

PI pilots sometimes work with their colleagues on
the ground to smoke out and arrest smugglers and
criminals. In 1953, about 14 miles north of Laredo,
Texas, on U.S. Highway 81, PIs Fred R. Loughmiller
and Norman Lau were checking traffic. They stopped
an automobile in which three men were riding, and
asked some routine questions.

Dubious about the answers given by one passenger
regarding his nationality, the inspectors searched the
car and found several guns. While the officers' attention was momentarily diverted, two of the three men
fled into brush alongside the highway.

Darkness finally forced the PIs to abandon their
search for the fugitives. They returned to base with
their one remaining suspect, leaving the other two
for searchers to track the next day. Early the next
morning a sign-cutting team went into action. Patrol
Pilot William F. Buckelew, with PI Lau as observer,
took off in a Patrol plane to help the ground crew.

The pilot found the men in the brush. Flying low over the hiding fugitives, PI Buckelew ordered them, by means of his loud-speaker, to raise their hands and walk back to the highway. One followed his orders; the other ran deeper into the brush. Buckelew followed the runaway, flushed him out, and herded him into the hands of waiting inspectors.

The pair admitted to taking part in eight car thefts in five states, and one of the fugitives had a .38 caliber pistol in his shoe. The third man proved to have been an accomplice in a San Antonio holdup.

6
A NIGHT ON THE DESERT

During a visit to the Border Patrol headquarters at Yuma, Arizona, I was invited one night to witness a train-check. I quickly accepted, for the train-check is one of the most interesting operations of the modern Border Patrol.

At midnight we drove off in a Border Patrol jeep, heading for a lonely spot in the desert alongside the railroad tracks. I rode out with Robert L. Jarratt, then Chief Patrol Inspector (or CPI) for the Yuma sector.

Climbing out of Jarratt's jeep, I stepped down onto the desert sands. Even at midnight, the sand still radiated warmth left over from the heat of day. Far to the east, a glow in the sky marked the city of Yuma. Near by, a coyote yelped.

We parked by the railroad, waiting for the westbound freight. Some of Jarratt's men rigged a booby trap—300 yards of 35-pound-test fishing line, stretching into the desert at right angles to the tracks.

"Sometimes a 'wet' will jump off the train and try to outskirt us," Jarratt explained. "Chances are he'll trip the line. When he does, he turns on that big floodlight, and we nab him."

Far down the track, the Cyclopean eye of the oncoming locomotive peered into the night. When the freight was nearly upon us, its engineer throttled down to a crawl—about the speed of a man's walk. A portable generator, parked at the side of the track by the Border Patrol, roared into life to feed two giant spotlights. These bathed the train with light on both sides.

With practiced agility, the inspectors jumped on and off the moving cars. Topside they ran along the narrow catwalks, lifting heavy hatches on the "reefers" or refrigerator cars to probe the cool interiors with long, silver flashlights. They squatted in the cinders to examine the underside of every car as the train clickety-clacked endlessly on.

"Time was we'd take 175 aliens off a single freight," said Jarratt. "Now we sometimes check 15 trains before we find a single wet. We perform this operation with 550 freights every month, day and night."

The radio in Jarratt's jeep crackled.

"Got tracks over here," said a voice with a soft Texas drawl. "One's got a half-moon heel plate, left shoe. Other's got heels with thirteen nail holes."

Jarratt turned down the volume.

"That's one of our jeep patrols, working the line near San Luis," he explained. "He's talking to another jeep team working with him and his buddy. They're sign cutting for tracks left by wets in the sand dunes."

Later we learned that the jeep crews had apprehended two line jumpers after chasing them for a mile into the Arizona sagebrush.

By now the train-check crew had probed every cranny of the eighty-car freight without turning up a single alien. Today this relentless night-and-day vigil practiced by the Border Patrol at Yuma is du-

Patrol Inspectors open the door to an ice compartment on a refrigerator car while checking for illegal aliens who might be riding freight trains to interior destinations.

plicated by Patrol units the entire length of the
frontier, from San Ysidro, California, to Brownsville,
Texas.

The train-check is a phase of one of nine categories
into which Border Patrol operations are divided.
These are river or line watch, sign cutting, city
patrol, traffic check (auto, plane, train and bus), anti-
smuggling, farm and ranch check, boat patrol, air
patrol, and intelligence.

For today's Border Patrol operations, the United
States is carved into twenty-two sectors. Nine Patrol
sectors lie along the Canadian border, ten along the
Mexican frontier. Two cover the southeastern section
of the United States, including Florida and the Gulf
Coast, and still another embraces Central California.
(There are 1,489 miles on the east coast and 1,293
miles on the west coast which are not under Border
Patrol supervision.)

Each sector is supervised by a Chief Patrol Inspector. He is aided by from one to three Assistant
CPIs, depending on the size of the operation. The
22 sectors are manned by some 1,700 officers, assisted
by some 400 auxiliary personnel. The latter group
includes electronic technicians, radio operators, auto-

mobile mechanics, clerks, detention guards and janitors.

The transportation fleet needed to move this small army includes autos, jeeps, trucks, station wagons, carryalls, buses, airplanes, patrol boats, outboard-motor craft of various designs, saddle horses and canoes.

Most patrol cars and all aircraft are equipped with two-way radios. Areas in which the Patrol operates are tied to a complex radio network which provides each sector with communication with its units and intercommunication between sectors. All sectors form part of the Immigration and Naturalization Service's nation-wide radio net. Within this highly efficient net, Border Patrol officers can communicate by voice between their bases and their patrol vehicles, boats or planes. The various sectors, from border to border and coast to coast, can relay strategic data to one another regarding movements of aliens and smugglers.

Though the Patrol is equipped with the most modern devices known to science, at times the PIs must rely on their wits to outmaneuver a smuggler or alien. One inspector grew tired of hearing repeated lies from aliens he apprehended, so he threw together a homemade "lie detector." Of course the gadget wasn't really a lie detector. The official polygraphs used by law-enforcement agencies throughout the world are extremely sensitive and complex devices, requiring the practiced eye of an expert to operate and interpret their findings.

Nonetheless, this inventive PI made a box and attached to it a mass of important-looking wires which were, in turn, linked to a series of buttons, buzzers and lights. Some of the wires (carrying no current) were fixed to the subject's arms. Then the PI would begin his questioning. As the alien responded, the PI would press buttons. Lights would flash, and buzzers would buzz. The alien, impressed by this wonderful box and certain it was probing into his innermost thoughts, would usually confess.

Another enterprising inspector fabricated an ingenious "alien detector" to help him on line watch in the desert. He rigged a fishline, tying one end to a bush and another to a trip switch on his flashlight. Whenever the light snapped on, another border jumper was nabbed.

Other officers used their wits to insure capture of aliens entering the United States over a bridge. The inspectors had found that, as soon as they commanded the lawbreakers to halt, the aliens would turn heel and flee back to their native land—and safety.

So the Inspectors stretched a stout length of clothesline across the bridge near the American end, fixing one end of the line shin-high to the bridge railing. This line they allowed to lie slack until the aliens began their flight back. Then the officers snapped the line tight and sent the fugitives sprawling. In seconds the invaders were under arrest.

7
PIs IN SNOWSHOES

Guarding America's southern boundary against alien invasion keeps hundreds of Patrol Inspectors on the move 24 hours a day, 365 days a year. But the Patrol also must keep a continual eye on another frontier, one of the world's longest undefended borders—the United States-Canadian boundary.

Controlling this 3,987-mile international line poses many a knotty problem for the Patrol. Extending from the State of Washington on the west to Maine on the east, the line traverses towering mountains, cuts across the vast, wind-swept plains of central Canada and the United States, as well as the Great Lakes, then twists and turns above New England until it dips into the Atlantic Ocean at Calais, Maine.

During many months of the year, vast reaches of this northern line are seized by the icy grip of winter. Temperatures plummet at times to forty degrees below zero, often lower. Blizzards, wilderness and swift rivers make travel through the area hazardous much of the year.

So, while inspectors on the southern line may be perspiring in the dry winter warmth of New Mexico, Arizona or Texas, the north-line PIs may be battling ten-foot snowdrifts, hampered by their heavy winter clothing and snowshoes. Their Mexican-border companions may be sign cutting in the sand dunes outside El Paso or roaming the cactus-dotted desert near Phoenix. But the northern PIs are more likely to be stalking aliens in the pine forests of New Hampshire or Vermont or running down flying bootleggers near Detroit.

And whereas the Mexican-line inspector uses Spanish constantly, the Canadian-border PI must, at times, be at home in that peculiar French-Canadian patois so commonly spoken in certain sectors of the

northeastern seaboard.

But whether he works in pine forests or sage brush, speaks French or Spanish, the Patrol Inspector's orders are the same: Find 'em, seize 'em, send 'em home.

The nine Border Patrol sectors located along the United States-Canadian line include twenty-four Patrol stations ranging from Calais, Maine, to Blaine, Washington. Exact statistics on the number of men deployed on United States frontiers are not available. One Patrol official explains why:

"Because the situation confronting the Border Patrol changes from time to time, it is necessary to shift our officer force and, on occasion, to open new stations and close old ones.

"For example," he continues, "the opening of the Great Lakes to large, ocean-going vessels when the St. Lawrence Seaway was completed created crewmen-control problems in an entirely new area."

So the Border Patrol is, and must always be, a flexible, fluid force.

Whether north or south, east or west, the Patrol Inspector is distinguished by the same uniform, the same jaunty campaign hat, and the same courage and devotion to duty. They regularly are required to

A view of the United States-Canadian boundary line stretching west near Eureka, Montana.

make split-second decisions on which may hinge, for them. life or death.

Such a decision was made by Curtis M. Thomson while he was on duty with the Grand Marais Border Patrol Unit in northern Minnesota. In April of 1957 word came through of the escape of three young gunmen from a United States Air Force prison in Jacksonville, Arkansas. Police in five states had thrown up roadblocks, and the latest intelligence indicated that the desperadoes were headed for the Canadian border in Thomson's area.

These were dangerous men. They had overpowered their guards, rifled a government safe, loaded themselves with stolen arms and ammunition, then stolen a car and headed north. En route, they picked up a hitchhiker.

The hitchhiker left the desperate trio when they abandoned their stolen car two miles south of the Canadian line in heavy woods near Thomson's station. He told his story to officials, who passed the word to the Border Patrol. Thomson armed himself with a sawed-off shotgun and, with another PI, started for the site on Grand Portage Trail where the car had been abandoned. They found the car in heavy woods, and Thomson immediately circled the area, cutting for sign of the fugitives. His comrade circled in another direction. Suddenly Thomson spotted the lawbreakers' trail, and called to the other Patrolman. By then, however, the other PI was too far away to hear his summons, so Thomson decided to trail the escapees alone. As he was then only two miles south of the international line, the PI feared the gunmen might escape into Canada if not apprehended immediately.

For some five miles, Thomson followed their fresh trail through the forest. It ended abruptly on the bank of the Pigeon River. The Pigeon, swollen by melting snows, was running deep. Their sign indicated the men had given up any idea of fording the Pigeon, and had headed down-river. Thomson pressed on. A mile downstream he came upon a large summer cabin, unoccupied by its owners at that season. Blinds had been drawn, so he could not see inside. But by silently listening at one of the windows, he believed he heard sounds of movement inside.

Thomson now faced a difficult decision, the kind which could result in his own injury or death. Should he return for help, or attempt to capture the criminals himself? The odds were against him.

He faced three armed fugitives who already had overpowered their guards, robbed a government safe, stolen weapons and run off with a car.

If he went for help, the fugitives might leave the cabin and flee into Canada before he returned. Thomson made his decision: he would take them single-handed.

Silently he tiptoed up to the cabin door. With his sawed-off shotgun at the ready, he seized the doorknob and swiftly opened the door. Thomson was in luck. All three gunmen, exhausted from their long flight, were asleep. Quietly he woke each one, disarmed each in turn, and took him prisoner. The lawbreakers' loot included three .45 automatic pistols, one .32 caliber pistol, five United States Treasury checks totaling nearly $200, one Postal Money Order for $30—all stolen from the Air Force Base at Jacksonville, Arkansas.

Thomson marched his captives downstream to the Pigeon River Port of Entry, where he turned both the prisoners and their loot over to the sheriff.

Flying contrabandists provide the Border Patrol with many problems along the Canadian line, just as they do along the southern frontier. Some may be hauling aliens into the states for a handsome fee. Others make lightning dashes from small, remotely located airfields into Canada and return with valuable cargoes of illegal liquor or other imports.

In two cases, inspectors employed their Patrol cars as weapons in battles with flying contrabandists. In one instance near Wyandotte, Michigan, PIs spotted a small craft coming in from Canada. Just as the plane touched ground, the PIs drove their car onto the field. The pilot, sensing danger, started feeding gas to his engine and raced down the field for a take-off. Determined not to let the pilot escape, the PI at the Patrol car's wheel drove his vehicle directly into the plane's take-off path. Wham! The plane smashed into the car, its propeller shattering the windshield and one door window. The terrific impact stunned the PIs inside the car for several moments. During those critical moments the pilot jumped from his wrecked plane, boarded another car which had meanwhile driven onto the field, and escaped.

But the stunned PIs rallied and jumped from their smashed car in time to seize the passengers abandoned in the plane—a Greek and a Rumanian who had been ferried across the line from Windsor, Canada. Their testimony later led to the capture of three other aliens. The passengers were tried, sentenced and deported. The plane—valued at $4,500—was seized by the government. But the fleet-footed pilot was never found.

In another case, PIs surprised a pilot unloading contraband liquor at a field near Plymouth, Michigan. The pilot, spotting the approaching PIs, climbed into his plane and attempted to take off. The PI driver maneuvered his car into the plane's path, but the aircraft bounced off the patrol car, taking off with a damaged wing.

The PIs found the plane in a farmer's field two miles away, where it had been abandoned. The pilot was never found, but the inspectors seized his plane and several cases of contraband liquor.

Among the slippery characters specializing in transporting aliens across the line was one Dominic Two-axe. His arrest followed the seizure of four Greek citizens, one each in Boston, Pittsburgh, Philadelphia and New York City. All had deserted their ships in Montreal, Canada. For a price they had been helped by a contrabandist to enter the United States without the proper documents.

Their testimony, and careful work by Patrol intelligence officers, led the trail to Dominic Two-axe, alias Grand Chief, alias Dr. Martin. Two-axe's favorite device was to make deals with Greek restaurant operators in Montreal. For a fee these men would spot Greek seamen who wished to enter the United States, and would lead the seamen to Two-axe.

A man with no conscience, Two-axe used his own children as decoys. He would drive his customers to Cornwall, Ontario, and there his accomplices would row the aliens across the St. Lawrence River to the United States. While this was going on, Two-axe himself would cross the line legally, in his car, accompanied by some of his many children. The number of children in the car always matched the number of customers being rowed across the river. Once on the American side, the youngsters would leave the car and the customers would take their places. Then Two-axe would haul the aliens deeper into the United States, and dump them. To enforcement officers, Two-axe's car always appeared to have the same number of occupants.

But the PIs saw through this ruse. They arrested Two-axe and took him to court, where he pleaded guilty and was given a two-year jail term.

While northern Patrol Inspectors stationed in cities

are performing their rounds in patrol cars, other PIs
may be working under much more rigorous conditions, deep in the woods. One particularly rugged
assignment has become an epic in the annals of the
Patrol.

In the heavy woods near Fort Kent, Maine, the
Patrol got word of a logging-camp operation where
some twenty-five or thirty Canadians were employed
illegally to cut a million board feet of lumber. The
camp lay deep in the forest wilderness near the
border, far from any large population center.

It was then mid-winter, with the mercury plunging
to 40 degrees below zero on occasion. Bone-chilling
winds, hip-deep snow and frequent rains made travel
through the forest hazardous. But the PIs decided
to raid the camp. They had to destroy the false
impression, widely held along the part of the line
known as Gagnon Ridge, that wilderness and cold
protected any alien who wanted to jump the line
to work illegally in the United States.

Four inspectors were assigned to the task. They
traveled by car from Fort Kent, and by train
and snowmobile to St. Pamphile, Canada. There

(Above) Inspectors on snowshoes patrol the border in northern Minnesota. (Below) A Border Patrol officer stands at the brink of the American Falls, checking the ice bridge which is forming across the river at
Niagara Falls. When the ice becomes solid, aliens may use it as an
avenue of illegal entry.

Canadian officials told them the "forest grapevine" already had picked up word of their coming. This demonstrated the efficiency of the grapevine, for the PIs had been sure that no one outside the Patrol knew of their plans.

Early on the morning of January 16, the four PIs mounted their snowshoes, slung their pack baskets on their backs, and set out along the International Boundary Slash toward Gagnon Ridge. For nearly five days, the four-man team battled the elements. Deep snow made trail breaking a nerve-wracking chore. First one inspector would break trail for fifty paces, to be spelled by a companion for the next fifty. At one point the terrain was so rugged each man was able to break only twenty paces before resting.

Heavy rains plagued their progress. The wet snow, clinging stubbornly to their snowshoes, soon made the men feel as if they were hauling steel anchors on each foot. Once they slogged along on top of a frozen river, the slush reaching their ankles. By night the men slept in some friendly forester's cabin, usually on a draft-swept floor.

On the fifth day the Inspectors spotted the Gagnon Ridge camp. After a careful surveillance, they made their raid and captured several aliens. Many of the invaders, alerted by the forest grapevine, already had fled into Canada. But enough arrests were made to awaken a healthy respect for the Border Patrol among those left behind.

This classic mission required four Patrol Inspectors to travel eighty-four miles on snowshoes in the depth of winter, risking their lives to exposure. They seized eight aliens, and questioned and released some sixty-five others. Many aliens, most of them aged or men with heavy family responsibilities, were released to avoid undue hardship, after they had given their solemn promise never to reënter the United States without documentation. The alternative was prison.

The logging-camp operator was convicted and fined, but his prison sentence was suspended to prevent hardship to his family.

The men of Gagnon Ridge, isolated by wilderness and weather, had felt convinced they were safe from the law. But they didn't know the men of the U.S. Border Patrol.

8
ONE IN A HUNDRED!

Although he can be as rough and ready as Jeff Milton when necessary, today's Border Patrol Inspector is more than a frontiersman. He is the product of careful selection and strenuous schooling.

"Of every 100 applicants for the job, roughly one survives," an official has reported.

Three hurdles face every applicant at the outset:

1. A written Civil Service examination, testing his intelligence and his aptitude for learning and adjusting to his new duties.

2. A searching oral examination, given him in person by three top-flight Immigration Service officials, including a Border Patrol Inspector.

3. A rugged physical inspection.

If he passes these, the applicant faces fourteen weeks of grueling study at the Border Patrol Academy, the West Point or Annapolis of the Patrol, at Port Isabel, Texas.

All applicants must be at least twenty-one years old (there is no maximum age limit). They must have a driver's license, and must have used it for at least a year.

On the physical side, these are some of the requirements:

1. Minimum height, 5 feet 8 inches (though the average is closer to 5 feet 10).

2. Weight, at least 140 pounds.

3. Vision, at least 20/40 without glasses, plus good color perception.

The minimum height requirement is based on psychology.

"We find that a man shorter than the minimum has more difficulty in his job," explained James F.

Greene, speaking as assistant commissioner in charge
of the Patrol. "There are a lot of characters loose
on this earth who think size and worth are one and
the same. So a small man in a police capacity now
and then has to prove he's a big man. This makes
for trouble.

'"But this certainly is no reflection on shorter individuals," he added.

The candidate's first hurdle is the written examination. If he passes, his name is placed on an eligible
list. His place on the list depends on the grade he
makes.

In time, he is called to an interview with the
oral examining board, usually in a major city near
his home. These men, in a kindly but firm fashion,
look him over. They judge him on these points:

1. Power of comprehension—can he "get
   the point" quickly?
2. Initiative and ingenuity—is he a self-
   starter, can he improvise in a crisis?
3. Judgment—will he make foolish mistakes, perhaps one which would cost his
   life or the life of a fellow officer?
4. Command of the English language—can

he write intelligent reports, can he communicate with others clearly?

They size him up as to physical appearance. Is he neat, clean? Does he handle himself like a real man? Does he show aggressiveness and willingness to assume responsibilities? In short, is he the kind of a man a fellow inspector could work with under trying circumstances?

In addition to a Border Patrol Inspector, the oral examining board includes a top-ranking official from two other Immigration Service divisions: Examinations and Investigations. All are interested in this new man, because all know that the Patrol is the man-power pool for the entire Immigration Service. They know that the candidate may, one day, be considered for a much more important post near the top.

Many applicants are eliminated at this stage. Those who survive the foregoing examinations are next subjected to a searching investigation to determine their general character and integrity, and their loyalty to the United States. As Border Patrol officers often are involved in operations which concern the national security of their country, these loyalty checks are most thorough.

If this phase of the investigation proves that the applicant uses liquor to excess, has shown disloyalty to the United States, has a poor moral record or has made "material misstatements" in his application, he will be rejected.

There are no specific educational requirements.

"We don't even require graduation from high school," one official explained. "But it stands to reason that good students will perform better in the Academy, and will show up better when promotions are made."

Despite the absence of any specific educational requirement, only two per cent of several recent Academy classes had not completed high school. And today the trend is more and more toward the college graduate. In one recent Border Patrol Academy class, twenty-nine men held college degrees. They represented a wide range of collegiate backgrounds, hailing from such well-known institutions as the University of California and George Washington University, and from many state colleges and universities.

Old-timers in the Patrol know from experience what qualities a new man must possess to make good.

"The basic attributes are loyalty and integrity,"

said James Greene. "If he hasn't these qualities, he doesn't fit in the Patrol. Then he must be industrious, cheerfully willing. In our work, the men may be called out all hours of the night and day. If you won't do a job willingly, you're not of much value. We haven't time to argue with a man every time there's a job to be done."

And he must be accurate.

"So much of our work hangs on what a man says, and what you say he says," Greene pointed out. "An officer's reporting must be accurate. If he can't · present the facts without coloring them, he is in trouble."

For those who meet the exacting requirements, the rewards can be rich.

"To start with, the beginning salary is good— better than many other jobs in the federal service," Greene stated. "Opportunities are unlimited. For the fellow who is willing to work, and is a little patient, there's no end of opportunity for advancement."

Greene himself is a good example. A Missouri boy, he joined the Patrol in 1941. He rose rapidly to become, at age 41, the chief officer in the Patrol and an Assistant Commissioner. Many of the Patrol's top-echelon officials are in their early or mid-forties.

In 1962 the trainee's basic salary was set at $5,540 a year. At the end of one year's service his pay was to be raised to $6,090 with provisions for within-grade increases up to almost $8,000. According to the 1962 amendment to the Classification Act, however, the basic pay for a man entering the Service would be raised to $5,795 in 1964. And Patrol Inspectors—men who had satisfactorily completed one year's service—would start at $6,390 and go up as high as $8,280. A Chief started at $11,150 in 1962, with provision for a range of from $11,725 to $14,805 by 1964. Except for the man just starting out on the job, all salaries depend on the number of years of service and the cumulative increases allowed within each grade, so there is considerable variation within one job level.

Officers also make "premium" pay for unscheduled overtime work. They may purchase low-cost life insurance, and enjoy special retirement privileges due to the hazardous nature of their work. To help them purchase the jaunty, forest-green uniforms which are their trademark, Inspectors receive an annual allowance of $100.

And the work is interesting.

"In this respect, I don't think there's any job that

can equal the Border Patrol," Greene said. "Scarcely a day passes that doesn't bring some new challenge. It's a job with plenty of variety."

Many PIs have gone on to important jobs in related fields. The present chiefs of two state police forces are former Patrol Inspectors. One officer was drafted, after World War II, to organize a border patrol for West Germany in coöperation with United States occupation forces in Europe. Another was requested by American occupation forces in Japan to set up a border patrol for that country and to advise Japanese authorities on alien-control procedures.

The job has its drawbacks, of course. Officers are expected to move around, and some individuals do not like this kind of nomadic living. They prefer to put down roots and stay in one community. Regular hours are impossible. Emergencies sometimes keep Patrol Inspectors on duty night and day for days on end. Officers may be detailed away from their home bases for weeks at a time. There is much night work, and exposure to extreme heat and cold is routine.

The element of physical danger is always present. Patrolmen frequently track down and arrest dangerous criminals, many of whom are armed to resist arrest at any cost.

New officers enter the Patrol on a "career-conditional" basis. The conditional period lasts three years, the first of which is a trial period. During this year the rookie is on probation and in training.

The fledgling officer is first assigned to work with seasoned veterans. These fellow officers make periodic progress reports on the quality of the newcomer's work. The reports are carefully studied by a panel of supervisory officers twice during the new man's first year.

If he fails to meet the requirements, he will be "separated" from the service. But if he survives the probationary period, at the end of the first year he is promoted from "Patrol Inspector Trainee" to "Patrol Inspector." Two years later his status is automatically converted from "career-conditional" to "career." He now has security of employment, and can make the Patrol a lifetime job if he wishes, provided he continues to perform to the Patrol's high qualifications.

The Patrol's rigid selection system inevitably leads to "survival of the fittest." It also insures a commendable *esprit de corps,* an atmosphere of loyalty and comradeship, which distinguishes the United States Border Patrol.

9
THE BORDER PATROL
ACADEMY

The Border Patrol Academy is one of the nation's most important law enforcement training schools. Since it was first set up in 1934 at El Paso, Texas, the Academy has turned out several thousand officers.

Now the school is located at Port Isabel, Texas, where all major Immigration and Naturalization Service training activities were brought together for the first time in 1961. Included in this educational program, known as the Officer Development Center, are the Border Patrol Academy, the Advanced Officers College and the Extension Training Unit. The facilities at Port Isabel, a former United States Navy installation, house the Academy in surroundings well suited to its needs. There are excellent living and dining quarters for students and instructors, a sufficient number of classrooms with the most modern teaching aids, and an ample amount of space for outdoor training activities. The 1600-acre tract even contains concrete runways and an airplane hangar. A Chief Patrol Inspector supervises the Academy.

Living quarters are furnished free to trainees. Two 2-story dormitories can each accommodate eighty-five men. Meals are supplied at cost to the trainee-students in a well-equipped dining hall. Trainees keep their own quarters clean and neat, giving them a thorough scrubbing every Saturday.

At the Academy the student works as he may never have worked before. By day, he attends lectures and demonstrations; by night, he studies.

The 14-week course includes 560 hours of instruction. Trainees attend classes eight hours daily, five days a week. One expert described the experience as equal to two years of college. Each trainee receives 204 hours of Spanish-language training, based on the most modern teaching techniques known. He also studies immigration and nationality laws, elementary rules of evidence, criminal law and court procedures, investigations and preparation of reports, Border Patrol operations, the care and use of firearms, finger-printing, methods of tracking law violators, jujitsu, physical training and first aid. There are also opportunities at Port Isabel for additional field training in ship inspection and boat patrol.

A course in Latin-American orientation gives the trainee an insight into the psychology and customs of the people with whom he will have most of his dealings. He learns valuable lessons in how to deal with the public, in courtesy, and in personal conduct.

New officers quickly get the feel of the Spanish language. Many of them will use it daily in their new careers. Some become so proficient they can fool the natives. Ed Niebuhr, as Assistant Chief of the Patrol, recalled an example:

"Another PI named 'Winnie' Baze and I were on the road north of Laredo one day, cutting sign on two aliens. They had zigged and zagged, and were hard to follow.

"Late in the afternoon we caught one of them coming out of a ranch house where he'd been looking for food. He was just about to make another circle.

THE BORDER PATROL ACADEMY

The Language Laboratory contains the most modern equipment for foreign language instruction. Here the students listen to Spanish recordings in individual booths; the instructor sits at the control console.

Trainees attend a class in immigration and nationality law. Movie and slide projectors and screens, charts and other up-to-date teaching aids are in constant use.

In addition to classroom work, the men participate in a vigorous physical education program.

We checked his shoes, and found he was one of the two we were following.

"We asked him where his partner was. He told us —they'll do that, because they don't like to go home alone. He said he'd agreed to meet his pal up at a windmill near by.

"So I went up to the windmill, and sat down under a mesquite tree. It hung down and shielded me from view. In about twenty minutes a straw hat bobbed up over a bush yonder, and then a head. He looks and looks, and then comes out from around the bush—just like a deer coming into a clearing.

"He'd decided everything was safe, so he stretched out on the sand to rest. I knew his name, so I called out, in Spanish:

" 'Ricardo. . . . Come here.'

"He called back: 'You come here. I'm too tired.'

"So I got up and walked over to him. He was lying there, with his hat pulled down over his eyes. I stood right next to him and said: 'Ricardo.'

"Slowly he lifted his hat. His eyes widened as he looked. Then he swore, in disgust: 'Caramba!' "

Academy instruction is highly practical, and the Academy has developed many of its own textbooks. One of these, *A Practical Spanish Grammar for*

Border Patrol Officers, has been reprinted numerous times.

Training does not end with graduation. Trainees take two difficult Spanish examinations during their first year of service, one after five months and the second after ten months on the job. At both points they are also tested on their knowledge of immigration law and procedure. If a trainee turns in a poor performance, or if his conduct and efficiency reports are unsatisfactory, he may be recommended for dismissal.

Resignations and washouts at the Academy are not uncommon. Most of those who fail are simply unwilling to put forth the necessary effort.

"This is not just an eight-hour job," said an Academy instructor. "Students who made a ninety average in high school and ranked near the top of their classes will rank in the bottom fourth here with an eighty-five average."

Though the PI is instructed to use his wits instead of his gun to gain his point, he knows how to use weapons when the occasion demands. Trainees at the Academy learn the art of marksmanship from recognized experts, who instruct them in the use of pistols, shotguns and rifles. For use in firearms instruction, a target range is located at some distance from the main buildings. Equipped to use both bull's-eye and silhouette targets, the range permits instruction of fifty trainees at one time.

Each man must later qualify quarterly with his service revolver, firing sixty rounds during these trials. A score of 335 to 394 of a possible 450 rates an officer as a Marksman. A score of 395 to 424 wins him an Expert's rating, while 425 or above distinguishes him as a Master.

Some of America's champion marksmen are officers in the Border Patrol, and Patrol pistol teams win top honors in national competitions year after year. The Patrol's proudest possession is the Colt Trophy, .45 caliber, which the Service now holds permanently. Patrol teams won it three years out of five.

In these matches, the Patrol fires against top marksmen from the Army, Marine Corps, Navy, Coast Guard, Air Force, and several state and metropolitan police force teams. Inspector Joe White shot on many of the winning teams, and was twelfth man in United States history to shoot 2600 out of a possible 2700. Inspector Bill Toney has won the national open championship, and Inspector Presley O'Gren became National Police Pistol Champion in 1960.

Patrol Inspector H. R. Mitchell, another instructor, became National Police Pistol Champion in 1962.

The men practice for these matches on their own time.

The .357 Magnum revolver is the most common arm carried by Border Patrolmen. This is equipped with a four-inch barrel. Inspectors are permitted, however, to carry a private firearm if they prefer, provided the weapon is of at least .38 caliber.

One of the Patrol's finest shots with a pistol is Inspector Bill Jordan, who for several years served as an instructor in the small-arms schools held annually at Camp Perry, Ohio, in connection with the National Matches.

10
"I HEARD BULLETS..."

Despite their prowess with firearms, Patrol Inspectors are taught to keep their revolvers holstered, and to use brains instead of lead whenever possible. Nevertheless they know how to use their firearms with telling effect when the occasion demands.

Many fierce gun battles have been fought between Patrol Inspectors and smugglers or border jumpers. In some of these, gallant Patrolmen have lost their lives or been seriously wounded. In others, their assailants have fallen.

Inspectors James Applewhite and Robert Coleman were patrolling the Rio Grande riverbank near Laredo, Texas, one night when they spotted a man crossing the river to the American side. As they squatted silently in the brush, waiting to halt the invader, they saw two more men enter the water on the Mexican side. As soon as the first alien hit the American shore, he emerged from the water and headed downstream. Coleman followed. Applewhite cautiously crept up on the other two as they came out of the water carrying their clothes above their heads.

While the men were dressing, Applewhite closed in. He told them they were under arrest for illegal entry, and identified himself as a Border Patrol officer. When he began to interrogate them, the men sat down on the sand of the riverbank.

In the darkness, Applewhite observed that they were moving their hands about under their legs. He flashed his light on them and ordered them to raise their hands.

Immediately the two men stood up. Applewhite found himself looking down the barrels of *three* pistols. One alien was brandishing a gun in each of his hands, while his companion was aiming a third weapon at Applewhite.

Then one of the invaders began firing, getting off two shots before turning to run toward the water. The other took aim at Applewhite, but before he could pull the trigger the Inspector shot and killed him instantly with a bullet near the left ear.

A veritable hail of lead filled the air then, as Applewhite engaged the fleeing alien in a running gunfight. Finally the fugitive dropped into the water some six feet from shore.

Meantime the third invader, running down the riverbank, was captured by Coleman. Coleman, dragging his captive, ran back to aid Applewhite. Turning his prisoner over to Applewhite, Coleman then waded into the stream to disarm the wounded alien and pull him to shore. The wounded captive later died, and the survivor scarcely merited survival. He was wanted in New Mexico in connection with the slaying, ten months earlier, of an entire family near Las Cruces.

Several of the Patrolmen slain in the line of duty have been victims of vicious ambushes. This was the fate of PI Thad Pippin.

Pippin and Inspector Egbert N. Crossett moved in on a band of liquor smugglers in the El Paso area across from Juarez, Mexico. The PIs had just arrested two Mexicans and seized two burros heavily loaded with contraband when friends of the arrested smugglers opened fire with sawed-off shotguns and pistols.

Pippin died with seven buckshot pellets in his body, all fired at point-blank range. Crossett was luckier. He was hit four times by pistol bullets, but all his wounds proved superficial.

Most of these perilous encounters end tragically, either for the Inspectors or their assailants. But a few of the Patrolmen's adventures have their funny side. One PI, lying in wait on a riverbank for approaching smugglers, fell off the bank and smashed, head-first, through the bottom of the smugglers' boat. When the PI surfaced, gasping for breath, a smuggler was waiting to whack him on the head with a paddle. Fortunately the smuggler's aim was poor.

In another comic adventure, two PIs broke down the door of a boathouse near Detroit to seize a smuggler. As they rushed through the door they fell ten feet into icy water. Taking advantage of the inspectors' awkward predicament, the smugglers threw their speedboat's engine into reverse, backed out of the boathouse, and escaped.

Inspectors sometimes play hunches which yield surprising hauls—and save their lives. One noon, Inspectors Robin S. Galaway and James B. Springer were checking traffic north of Laredo. The driver, though apparently a United States citizen, seemed nervous and hesitant under questioning. So they ordered him to the side of the road and searched his car. In the glove compartment, the officers found a loaded .25 caliber pistol. Four more loaded revolvers were found hidden elsewhere in the car. The driver had $2,500 in his pockets. But when questioned he refused to make any statement to the inspectors.

They took him to Border Patrol headquarters. There he was identified, from an FBI bulletin, as Earl "Killer" Smith, wanted by the Federal Bureau of Investigation for robbery of the Andrews Air Force Base Bank at Washington, D.C. His capture helped FBI agents to track down two other members of his gang.

Narrow escapes are almost everyday affairs in the Patrol. One PI had his wristwatch band shot off in an exchange of bullets. Another was nearly run down

Disguised as a civilian boat operator and female companion, two Border Patrol officers watch aliens entering the United States illegally across the St. Lawrence River. When the aliens land, the inspectors will shed their civilian clothing, revealing the regulation uniforms worn underneath.

by a carload of Cubans when the PI thwarted their
plan to take off, illegally, from a Gulf Coast airfield.
The officer was moving in on an old B-18 that was
being loaded on a small Florida airstrip for a flight
to Cuba with arms and rebels. As the PI closed in
on the plane, a car shot out of nowhere and headed
straight for the officer. As it bore down on him, the
PI shot at the car's front tires with his submachine
gun. The Cubans came pouring out of the car in
a hurry, their hands up.

In another close scrape involving Cubans, a Border
Patrol launch overtook a boat carrying Cuban rebels
in United States waters. One of the islanders tossed
a hand grenade aboard the Patrol craft, but the
grenade miraculously failed to explode. Had it
detonated, the grenade would have set off several
cans of confiscated black powder stacked on the Patrol
vessel's deck, and wiped out the launch and its crew.

Another PI owes his life to his assailant's ignorance
of firearms. On Patrol duty in the Gulf of Mexico,
this PI stepped aboard a foreign ship suspected of
carrying undocumented aliens. A young man aboard
ship jammed a machine gun into the officer's stomach
and pulled the trigger.

There was a deadly click, but no explosion. The

PI's assailant had failed to feed the first round into the chamber when he loaded the magazine into the machine gun.

In reporting such hair-rising incidents, inspectors sometimes are surprisingly modest. One wrote, after living through a vicious gunfight:

"I heard bullets in close proximity to my person."

Though they stick close to the rulebook when it comes to law enforcement, PIs sometimes are called upon to interpret the law to fit the circumstances when human life is at stake.

In a raid on a band of smugglers, one PI seized four rifles. He was asked by one smuggler under what law the PI was authorized to seize the arms. The officer replied:

"The law of self-preservation."

No one, then or later, questioned his wise interpretation of the rules.

11
HOW TO OUTSMART
AN INDIAN

Equipped with the last word in electronic gadgets, aircraft and armament, the Border Patrol is as modern as tomorrow. But one important activity of the modern Patrol relies on an ancient art, older than the oldest American Indian. This art is called "sign cutting."

Any alien who jumps our border to enter the country illegally will, inevitably, leave some sign of his entry. It may be a candy wrapper or cigarette butt, thoughtlessly cast aside. It could be an overturned stone, a footprint, a branch snapped from a bush. Whatever the sign, it can be cut or detected by a trained sign cutter.

The term "cut" has an interesting origin. Sometimes a tracker will lose the sign of the man he is following. To find it again, he will walk—or drive—in a great circle, attempting to "cut" the man's tracks again. Hence, sign cutting.

Most PIs are capable sign cutters; many are acknowledged experts whose services are in great demand. Special instruction is given in the art to all new officers at the Border Patrol Academy. On entering the Patrol, some officers already are experienced sign cutters. Perhaps as farm boys they learned to cut sign in tracking down a lost cow or horse. Or as hunters they taught themselves the skill while stalking their game.

Once practiced by all Indians and frontiersmen, sign cutting was nearly lost as an art for a time. Then the Border Patrol revived it, and made sign cutting a part of the professional bag of tricks of today's Patrol Inspector.

One PI, Merritt Shiveley, is so good at sign cutting that his fellow officers swear he could "track an ant across a flat rock." Other PIs have become so skilled that they would force an Apache Indian scout to blush in shame.

As a matter of fact, this actually happened during World War II. After the United States declared war on Hitler's Germany, many German citizens then living in our country were placed in internment camps for the duration of the war.

One of these camps was located in the rugged mountains near Fort Stanton, New Mexico. It adjoined the Mescalero Apache Indian Reservation.

Nearly 500 Germans were confined in this internment camp, which was placed under Border Patrol supervision. Many attempts were made by the internees to escape, but all failed until one morning at roll call three Germans failed to answer the roll.

The camp was searched, and inspectors found that the trio had dug a tunnel. It started inside a tool shed, burrowed under the high fence, and emerged behind a horse corral outside the compound—a distance of some seventy-five feet.

Expert Border Patrol sign cutters were immediately ordered from the El Paso, Texas, sector to help track down the fugitives. But officials knew it would be some time before these cutters could reach the camp. So they decided, meantime, to ask Indians from the

Mescalero Reservation to help in the search.

Three Apaches hit the trail about an hour before the Border Patrol sign cutters arrived from El Paso. The Patrolmen, striking out after the Germans, almost immediately picked up their sign and followed them for thirty-six hours through forbidding country. And they got their men!

Meanwhile, nothing was heard from the Indians. A check was made at the reservation, but no one had heard from them, or seen them return. So the Patrol sign cutters started out after the Apaches.

They cut the Indians' sign and followed them for twelve hours. At last they found them wandering through some woods, sad, hungry—and lost! The Apaches were, by then, nearly three miles away from the trail left by the escaping Germans.

Tracking invaders through desert and mountain country is exhausting, demanding work. Many times, PIs will remain away from home or base for days, pursuing an alien.

While in charge of the Chula Vista, California, sector, Inspector Bill Davis received a phone call from Mrs. Fayet Clark, wife of one of his men. Mrs. Clark said she was a little worried because her husband had been gone nearly four days on a sign-

cutting mission.

Inspector Davis asked Mrs. Clark why she had waited so long to report Clark's absence. (Because Clark was stationed in an outlying post, distant from the base, he operated independently.)

"Oh, it's not unusual for Fayet to be out of touch when he's cutting sign," she said. "But after three days, I begin to worry."

It turned out that Clark and his partner, Frank Bray, were safe. However, they had found five aliens in the wild Laguna mountains. The terrain was so rugged that they had been forced to cut and re-cut the aliens' sign many times before finally locating them.

Whether he is patrolling the pine forests of the Canadian border or ranging the hot, barren reaches of New Mexico and Texas, the PI learns to recognize sign almost by instinct. He looks first, of course, for the obvious—evidence of a campfire, a trampled plant, a cigarette butt. But he learns, too, to rely on a sixth sense that warns him something is not quite normal. This super-sense can caution him of the nearness of a smuggler or an alien on the run.

In Texas one day Inspector Miles J. Scannell was

A Patrol Inspector on foot has found the remains of a cooking fire where illegal aliens stopped to eat. He calls his partner, in a nearby jeep, by walkie-talkie radio.

driving down a highway chatting with a PI teammate. (Scannell, one of the Patrol's best sign cutters, had joined the Patrol after years of punching cattle in the Big Bend region of Texas.) Suddenly Scannell brought his car to a stop. He gazed attentively at a dagger plant—a kind of cactus—near the roadside. Something was wrong with that plant, and Scannell was puzzled.

Examining the plant more closely, Scannell found that the sharp-pointed tip of the "dagger" had been broken off and laid horizontally across the plant's top as if to form a pointer. Noting where it pointed, Scannell walked to a small clump of brush about a hundred yards away. Inspecting the clump, Scannell found a large cache of contraband liquor concealed in the bushes!

The average man, untrained in the art of sign cutting, doubtless would have passed the plant without a second glance.

Through years of experience, top-flight cutters have learned many tricks. Though sign cutting may be practiced twenty-four hours a day, experts have found that the best time is early in the morning, when sign is freshest.

They have found, too, that tracks can be seen most

plainly from an angle. So they shift their line of vision, looking at the ground from different angles. And they have learned that tracks can best be seen when the sun is low (casting greater shadows), and when glare is at a minimum.

The seasoned sign cutter learns to distinguish quickly between fresh and old tracks. He may note, for example, that a lizard has slithered across a track, or a snake has left its smooth trademark over a print. Perhaps it has rained since the track was laid down. Knowing when it last rained, he can put an approximate "age" on the evidence. Also, if he knows the habits of local wildlife, he can make an intelligent deduction on the time element. Certain animals come out only at night, while others are daytime prowlers. Their tracks, when mingled with those of an invader, will give the sign cutter valuable clues.

Rats, in sandy sections, will travel in warm weather as long as the moon shines. In cold weather, or when there is no moon, they travel only during the early part of the night. The little desert lizard apparently crawls from his sandy bed at crack of dawn, and busily makes sign all day long.

In many instances, it is extremely difficult for a PI to determine when a track was laid down. In desert regions of the Southwest, a track may remain fresh-appearing for days. On the other hand, at certain seasons of the year when the wind kicks up the sand, or moisture is in the air, very accurate deductions can be made on the sign's probable age.

So the experienced sign cutter becomes a student of nature, an amateur weather forecaster, an expert in desert lore. When he goes on duty, he talks with his colleagues of the previous shift. He will ask them, for example, if and when the wind blew. Was there any rain? When did the dew settle? The answers to these and other questions may help him to evaluate sign he will cut during his hours on duty.

If the PI finds rocks that have been displaced or grass which has been trampled, or if he notes tracks on very hard ground, he may conclude that something or someone has passed a given point very recently. He knows that rocks which have been moved from their ancient sites very soon take on the appearance of surrounding rock. Grass which has been stepped on will rapidly spring back to its normal state. And tracks on hard ground fade rapidly. These things, experience has taught him.

(Above) A seasoned sign cutter follows tracks in a region west of El Paso which has long been a favorite route of travel for illegal entrants. (Below) A Patrol Inspector leaves his jeep to look for tracks of illegal aliens along the International Border near San Ysidro, California.

It is demanding work, but exciting.

"Sign cutting matches the hunter against the hunted," one veteran PI observed. "It's the most challenging kind of hunt imaginable. It is one man's wits against another's. The lawbreaker knows he is being tracked—or may reasonably assume that he is —and he makes the job just as difficult as possible for his tracker."

12
A BATTLE OF WITS

To throw Border Patrol sign cutters off their scent,
border jumpers have gone to almost unbelievable
extremes.

The less inventive have walked on leaves or grass,
jumped from rock to rock, or brushed out their
tracks with tumbleweeds or brush. Others, more
imaginative, have crossed dirt roads on stilts, or with
burlap bags wrapped around their feet. One border
jumper put horseshoes on his feet and walked north
for miles, only to run smack into two PIs sitting

quietly in the brush, waiting to corral their "horse."

Another carved cow hoofs from wood and fixed them to his sandals. He was tracked down and arrested by an officer who knew perfectly well there was no such creature as a two-legged cow. The same trick was tried by a pair of aliens who attached crossed sticks to their feet and attempted to imitate cow tracks. The inspectors caught up with the "cows" just as they were removing their false feet. This pair—making four tracks—might have escaped detection except for the fact that one PI, an old hand in the area, knew there were no cows in his sector.

To the untrained eye, most footprints look much alike. But expert sign cutters like Senior Patrol Inspector Jim Dove can read a lot of information in the impression left by a shoe or foot in dirt or sand. They can tell something about the wearer's general size, height and weight. They even know if he limps. His prints also will reveal whether the wearer was running or walking. Or walking backwards!

One day, in the soft Imperial Valley sands near El Centro, California, SPI Dove spotted a set of prints —and knew he had something. The prints *appeared* to be headed for Mexico. But Dove knew better. He knew that men walking backwards leave telltale evidence. Their heels dig in, making deeper impressions than are left by a man walking forward. The toe, at the same time, makes a lighter imprint than it would in normal, forward movement.

So Dove trailed the prints north, into the United States, for more than a mile. All this time the prints headed south, toward Mexico. The trail led across rocks, into a plowed field, and seemed to come to a dead end on a paved sidewalk.

This would have stopped many a sign cutter, but not Dove. He tracked the prints *along a paved sidewalk* to the rear of a house. There he found not one man—but *two*—and took them in.

Dove had known he would find two men. For he had deduced, after following the trail a short time, that two fugitives were involved. The smaller man had gone first, walking backwards; the second and larger alien had followed, stepping into the prints of his comrade.

Apart from efforts to fool the sign cutters, aliens and smugglers have resorted to the most imaginative tricks in their attempts to enter the country illegally. One smuggler was picked up at Livermore, California, with a girl draped across the motor of his car. At the smuggler's trial, his defense lawyer argued

that the girl could not possibly have been transported in this fashion. Obviously there wasn't room enough under the hood for such a trick. He implied that the Border Patrol had made up this fantastic story to convict the smuggler.

So a Border Patrol officer got under the hood. The hood was slammed shut, and the car was driven ten miles with the officer riding—very uncomfortably— over the hot, smelly motor. Verdict: guilty as charged.

Aliens have been found suspended from the ceilings of boxcars, and buried under loads of coal with their faces blackened to match their hiding places. Others have concealed themselves in loads of hay or lumber, hogs or sugar beets. They have had themselves shipped across the line in an amazing variety of containers, ranging from piano crates to coffins.

One was found aboard a truck in a pickle barrel. Still another crossed the line with a circus, hiding in the hayrack in a giraffe's cage.

Aliens have bought, borrowed or stolen United States military uniforms, crossing the line disguised as soldiers, sailors or marines. Some have purchased

A Patrol officer checks the abutments of railroad bridges across the Niagara River Gorge. A favorite trick of aliens is to enter the United States illegally by descending from bridges, then following trails from the Gorge to streets of Niagara Falls, New York.

surplus army camouflage suits for crossings in the desert, hoping thus to blend in with the terrain.

One especially inventive team bought gym suits and pasted numbers on the fronts and backs of their sweat shirts. They then mounted bicycles and pedaled north from the Mexican border toward San Francisco. To the casual observer, they were merely contestants in a cross-country bicycle race. They nearly got to the Golden Gate city before a PI, suspecting a trick, unmasked and arrested them.

Smugglers have built false beds in their trucks and false compartments in their automobiles to accommodate customers.

"Any place big enough to get into, they'll get into," one officer commented.

"We kept hearing about a certain smuggler bringing in aliens," he related, "but we could never catch him with the goods. Finally we got some solid intelligence and were ready for him.

"He drove up to the line, big as life, with 600 pounds of fish. He had crossed many times before in this iced truck. This time we checked very carefully, and found he had built a compartment under the truck. In it were four aliens, all very wet—and slightly fishy."

Veteran inspectors thought they had seen everything until they witnessed a smuggling incident
which occurred in New Mexico. They had picked
up an alien, and asked him how he made his entry
into the United States. He told officers he had been
smuggled across the line and placed with twelve other
aliens inside the tank of a sprinkler truck. There,
he said, he and his companions had spent the night.
The next day the smugglers had given each alien
a pint bottle of water for drinking. They were then
driven more than 200 miles across the desert of New
Mexico to a farm area in the middle of the state.

This seemed a ridiculous story. It was then mid-
summer in New Mexico, where the officers knew that
temperatures sometimes soared to 120 degrees in the
sun. They believed that the heat from the sun, beating
on the metal tank of the sprinkler truck, would cook
anyone inside.

There were only two sprinkler trucks in that area.
So the PIs arranged a stake-out (an innocent-looking
or hidden observation post), which permitted the captured alien to observe, from hiding, each of the trucks
with its driver. He identified one of these as his
smuggler. Under interrogation, the driver confessed
his guilt. His truck was brought to Border Patrol

headquarters and examined. In full sunlight, a thermometer was suspended inside the tank. It broke after hitting 130 degrees Fahrenheit.

The bottom of the tank had been lined with sand, which was then soaked with water. Sand and water had been put in the tank, the driver explained, so that water would drip slowly from sprinklers at the rear. This would give the offhand impression that the truck was in normal operation. But inside the tank, under the boiling sun, the water created the effect of a super-Turkish bath, with temperatures ranging from 130 degrees upward.

The driver said he had checked with a thermometer during one of his cross-desert runs, and found that the heat did not go beyond a maximum of 140 degrees Fahrenheit as long as the truck was in movement. Once, with thirteen aliens aboard, his truck had had a flat tire in the desert. Before the smuggler could change it, six of the thirteen had fainted. But he boasted that all recovered as soon as the truck began to roll again.

Apprehension of this smuggler touched off a chain reaction which ended with the arrest of some 150 aliens and closed one of the Border Patrol's most bizarre cases.

13
INTELLIGENCE—A SPECIAL KIND OF "SIGN"

While their fellow officers are tracking down clues in the desert or mountains, other PIs are working with another kind of sign in the Patrol's relentless drive against invaders. This special brand of sign is called "intelligence." Today each Patrol sector has an intelligence officer. His rank—equal to that of Assistant Chief Patrol Inspector—is a measure of his importance. The Border Patrol Academy includes in its curriculum a special course covering the gathering and interpretation of intelligence.

The Border Patrol established its own intelligence or information-gathering organization in 1955. It was charged with obtaining information which would help inspectors to apprehend smugglers and control the movement of aliens across our borders.

How does it work? Take the case of the two Chinese crewmen who jumped their ship at Mobile, Alabama. They had worked out a neat plan to enter the country illegally. They figured that, by taking a plane to New York, they would be swallowed up among the countless millions of inhabitants in the big city.

But the Chinese did not know that the Border Patrol had its own intelligence network, organized specifically to thwart such plans as theirs. Alerted to the fact that the Chinese had abandoned the ship, officers in Mobile went into action. By analyzing all possible means of escape, they discovered that the Chinese had only one choice for a quick departure: a nonstop flight to New York. So they phoned ahead, and arranged for a reception committee.

The Chinese walked off their plane, straight into the arms of waiting officers!

Patrol intelligence officials are familiar with the culture and customs of the country adjacent to their sector, and speak its language fluently. They maintain files of charts, maps and statistics which provide them with a continuous and immediate estimate of the situation. They also build lists of smugglers, smuggling activities and methods, and informants.

Fellow inspectors, on their rounds, gather information which is turned over to an intelligence officer for analysis. A Patrol pilot, for example, may spot a large group of people massed on or near the Mexican side of the frontier. This information is intelligence, and is passed on for examination. Acting on the pilot's tip, officials in that sector may deploy extra men to that area in anticipation of an attempted flood of illegal entries.

Intelligence officers watch for any change in economic conditions in areas near the frontier. If a flood or drought leaves heavy crop damage in its wake, many farmers in the stricken zone may be forced to seek employment away from home. This may lead to efforts to jump the border. Likewise, a newspaper story reporting dramatic population growth in towns on or near the frontier is Patrol intelligence. A population increase of ten percent in a town close to the line increases the probability of illegal aliens by ten percent, perhaps more.

Along the St. Lawrence River on the United States-Canadian frontier, officers may be alerted by residents to the fact that ice bridges are forming at certain points. This is intelligence, and such locations are plotted on a map and watched to prevent the use of such bridges for illegal entries.

Intelligence officers carefully chart the number of border jumpers who slip through the Patrol's tight cordon along the line, and who are picked up later in the interior. They also note the number who are caught, and when and where.

Maps are prepared from these statistics, permitting intelligence officers to predict the probable movements of aliens in the future. They have noted over the years, for example, that Mexican aliens tend to follow certain patterns of movement, favoring certain railroads and highways. This intelligence permits closer controls on the areas of heaviest traffic, and justifies relaxed vigilance in less traveled zones.

All Border Patrol officers, like their fellow law-enforcement officers in other branches of police work, have contacts who furnish information which might lead to the arrest of violators. The Patrol is authorized, by law, to pay for information. Many contacts work without pay, of course. Some do accept pay-

An automobile crosses an ice bridge that has formed across the St. Lawrence River at Clayton, New York. Border Patrolmen must watch such bridges to make sure they are not used for illegal entry.

ment for their services, and the term "informant" is used for these individuals. The capture of many smugglers and aliens has been brought about through information supplied by informants and contacts.

In recent years there has been a steady increase in the ownership of small, private aircraft. And the range of some of the planes has been extended considerably. Hundreds of makeshift airstrips are available to small-plane operators along the entire length of the United States-Mexican frontier. Air-borne smugglers, flying low, can operate from any number of these hidden fields.

Because the ground forces of the Border Patrol have been able to make it extremely difficult for aliens to enter illegally on foot, by car or other ground conveyance, smuggling activity by air has increased. To control it, the Patrol must pay special attention to the gathering of information which relates to the movements of private aircraft.

A tip from one informant led to an unusual haul in California. Patrol intelligence officers received word from one of their sources that a war-surplus BT-13 aircraft would be flown from a Mexican field with an odd cargo: 130 parrots! Analyzing the possible flight plans the pilot might follow, the officers placed a stake-out at the San Bernardino airport.

Sure enough, the contrabandists landed at San Bernardino. The birds, valued at $8,200, were seized and destroyed. A United States law prohibits the importation of parrots because they often carry a powerful virus called psittacosis.

The Patrol doesn't catch all smugglers, of course, despite its well-organized intelligence network. "With all that real estate to cover, the odds are against our getting 'em all," one Intelligence man observed. "But it's our job to make sure that we get as many of 'em as humanly possible."

14
PARAKEETS, LOBSTER TAILS—AND PEOPLE

Trans-border smuggling operators concentrate on three commodities: narcotics, liquor and human beings. In his role as Border Patrol Inspector, the PI is empowered primarily to deal with the criminals who traffic in fellow humans.

But under special circumstances he may handle cases connected with the smuggling of narcotics and other merchandise. Under law he carries dual authority, being designated a "Customs Patrol Inspector" to handle special cases. For this he receives no extra compensation.

As a Customs Patrol Inspector, the PI may arrest smugglers of nonhuman contraband if such smugglers are encountered while the PI is discharging his regular duties as a Border Patrolman. Such cases arise frequently.

Mexico has long been a major source of contraband narcotics. Marijuana and heroin, "goofballs" and other drug items may be purchased with relative ease in certain Mexican border towns. These frontier cities also are concentration points for drug smugglers.

It is a flourishing, vicious racket. A highly successful narcotics dealer with—at times—millions of dollars at stake has no regard for human life. He will cheat, lie, steal or kill without the slightest pang of conscience.

PIs, who have a special hatred for the dope smuggler, at times can literally smell him coming. One night in Del Rio, Texas, patrolmen were making a routine road check. They stopped a car to check its passengers for nationality. One man offered a tattered, soiled birth certificate as evidence of United States citizenship.

The PI unfolded the document and laid it flat on the hood of the car, shining his flashlight on the paper. While he was reading, he smelled—mingled with the warm gasoline fumes rising from the hood —the telltale aroma of marijuana. To those who know this odor, there is no mistaking it.

The PI opened the hood. There was the forbidden marijuana, neatly packed in plastic bags and draped around the motor.

Playing a hunch led PIs to the capture of another big haul. Inspectors stopped a car and found they had stopped a smuggler with a carful of liquor.

"Okay, boys," said the smuggler. "You've got me. Let's go."

But the Inspectors, sensing something bigger was afoot, decided to stick around. The smuggler seemed too anxious to leave. Their hunch paid off. Within an hour, a big truck came rumbling down the same road. It was crammed with contraband liquor—and owned by the same smuggler.

Though liquor and drugs figure first among contrabandists, many other items are moved in transborder smuggling operations. The variety is endless, ranging from parakeets to lobster tails, and from Swiss watches to tungsten ore. Hay smuggling enjoyed a brisk traffic for a period in the northeastern

United States. At that time, Canadian hay could be sold at prices far below the prevailing United States market.

In recent years, smuggling by air has given the Border Patrol and Customs authorities a new set of headaches. One Mexican smuggler, Felix Vivas, once boasted he had made 250 illegal flights from Mexico to the United States over a three-year period.

Planes have been seized flying into California with loads of abalone, a sea-food delicacy much favored on the West Coast. One alien pilot was captured in Las Vegas, Nevada, during a futile attempt to smuggle in two tons of abalone for the plush restaurants of that gambling resort. Still another pilot was caught with 800 pounds of chile from neighboring Mexico.

Traffic was brisk for a time between Florida and Cuba. One Piper Apache was seized at Kendall, Florida, when an alien pilot landed with two Cubans and approximately $200,000 in Cuban currency. But the oddest seizure took place in the Tucson, Arizona, sector.

Border Patrol Inspectors there grabbed a twin-engined Cessna as it landed with about 2,000 pounds of tungsten ore. The cargo was valued at $3,500.

Questioning the pilot, they found he had made five earlier trips from Mexico with the same contraband.

They were puzzled. Why would the smuggling of a heavy commodity like this prove profitable by air?

Checking, they found that Mexican ore could be flown in and sold profitably by undercutting the price then asked for the same ore by United States mines. The pilot could purchase a plane-load in Mexico for $1,200, selling it across the line for three times the purchase price.

Often the smuggler will attempt to get rid of the evidence before he is seized. PIs David L. Seeburger and Harvey L. Perry were checking traffic fourteen miles east of Laredo, Texas, one night when such an attempt was made.

They stopped a car containing four men, one in the back seat. PI Seeburger, checking this passenger, flashed his light on the floor of the car. He spotted two large boxes under the man's legs.

"What's in the boxes?" he asked.

There was no reply. So he ordered the driver to pull over to the side of the road. The driver moved slowly ahead as if to obey, then suddenly picked up speed and shot eastward. Seeburger and Perry immediately gave chase in their patrol car, with red light flashing and siren wailing. As they closed in, the inspectors saw two boxes being thrown from a window of the car. Finally, four miles from the check point, they halted the runaway.

One of the passengers admitted he had tossed the boxes from the speeding car and said they contained marijuana. PI Seeburger radioed Border Patrol headquarters for help in locating the jettisoned contraband.

Fellow officers found the boxes. They held narcotics valued at $14,000, based on the market price for marijuana then current in Chicago. Most such seizures are valued in thousands of dollars. A recent one, in the Chula Vista sector, included 43 pounds of marijuana cigarettes, which would have sold for approximately $20,000.

Smugglers will not hesitate to double-cross their customers. PIs tell about a recent case in which two Americans collected fees from six Mexican aliens, agreeing to haul them deep into the interior of the United States. Here the Mexicans hoped they could find employment.

But the treacherous American smugglers arranged to be "intercepted" near the border by confederates

who flashed a red spotlight on them as they approached with the aliens. The aliens were told that
they were in danger of being seized by the "migras"
(as Mexicans call Immigration Service officials), and
ordered to hide in the brush. The smugglers said
they would decoy the Patrolmen from the scene, then
return for their customers.

Of course they never returned. The aliens were
left stranded. Driven by hunger and thirst, they
finally abandoned their hiding place and were picked
up by the Patrol.

Fortunately the treacherous smugglers were arrested, found guilty, and sentenced.

Another, even more heartless double-cross was per-
petrated by a Mexican smuggler against his own
countrymen. This despicable character gathered a
group of would-be wetbacks, took their fees, and
escorted them to the Mexican side of the Rio Grande.
There he ordered them to strip, and to hand their
clothing and possessions to him for "safe conduct"
to the American side in a boat. He then told them
to swim to the United States side.

The smuggler crossed in a skiff, his customers following in his wake. Just before the smuggler hit the
shore, one of his confederates—planted in the bushes

—shouted, "Alto [halt]. This is the Border Patrol."

Immediately the smuggler shouted to his country-men to return to Mexico to avoid capture. They, of course, obeyed. The smuggler then landed on the United States side. His confederate joined him from the bushes, and they split the poor refugees' money, clothing and belongings.

To outwit such diabolical cunning takes resource-ful thinking. In an amazing feat of impersonation, Inspector Kenneth T. Fine displayed such thinking.

Fine, then on duty at Brawley, California, had for some time been watching an alien-smuggler named Lew Hampton. Hampton had been tried and con-victed for bringing in Mexicans, and released on bond pending retrial. Fine knew Hampton's methods, and knew he worked with a woman accomplice named Betty White. One night, fellow officers got a tip that Hampton and Miss White were planning to smuggle a batch of aliens into the country. They tailed Hampton's car to the outskirts of Indio, Cali-fornia.

Alerted to the development, Fine drove to the ranch of one Joe Duran. Fine knew this ranch was the base for Hampton's operations. As he neared it, Fine saw people milling around in a date grove.

Driving into the grove, he turned out his lights, blew his horn, stepped out of his car, and whistled. He knew this was the sequence followed by Hampton.

The night was dark. So as the waiting aliens swarmed into his car, they did not observe that Fine was wearing a Border Patrol uniform. One alien even tried to get into the trunk!

"Come on," another called to Fine in Spanish. "Let's get out of here, before the 'migras' catch us."

"Where am I supposed to take you?" Fine asked, in Spanish.

"Bakersfield," one replied.

"How much are you supposed to be paying me?"

"Fifty-five dollars apiece," was the reply.

"Who made the arrangements?" Fine continued.

"Joe Duran," one answered.

Then Fine asked: "Who is supposed to be hauling you?"

"An Americano and an American woman," he was told. "Let's get out of here before the 'migras' come."

Fine decided it was time to reveal his identity. He turned on the car's lights, which revealed him plainly as one of the feared "migras."

"And who do you think has you now?" he asked the astounded Mexicans.

Then Fine, using shrewd judgment, decided to ask his astonished prisoners to help him catch the very smuggler he was impersonating. After a great deal of chattering and waving of arms, the aliens agreed.

"What does it matter? We're caught anyhow," one commented. "We might as well have some fun."

So Fine and his companions drove to a neighboring village from which he telephoned to Indio, asking a fellow PI to bring him a change of clothes—and a Mexican-style straw hat. Fine dressed in these, and found he blended nicely—the night was so dark— with his Mexican partners-in-crime.

Fine's PI colleague then drove the officer-turned-alien and his five Mexican companions back to Duran's date grove. There Fine and his companions returned to their hiding place to wait for Hampton.

In time, the smuggler drove up. Noting there were six men in the waiting group, Hampton said: "I can carry only five."

Quickly Fine shoved one Mexican from the group into the shadows. Then Hampton asked for their money.

"We'll give it to you when we reach Indio," one Mexican replied.

"We're not going through Indio," Hampton told

them. "I was arrested there once by the 'migras' and I'm afraid to go back."

A spirited argument followed between Hampton and the Mexicans, Fine throwing in an occasional word. Finally Hampton told his clients the trip was off until the following night. Miss White drove up in a second car, and Hampton told her they were leaving.

At this point, Fine pulled his flashlight and pointed it at Hampton and Miss White. Hampton, seeing clearly that Fine was no Mexican, began to plead for leniency.

Both Hampton and Miss White were duly turned over to authorities, and Fine's Mexican accomplices were processed and deported.

15
SEARCH ALL PRISONERS!

Today, as in the rough-and-ready times of six-shooter justice, Border Patrolmen must be tough to get their badges. They must be even tougher to keep them.

Some years ago the Mutual Life Insurance Company of New York made a survey of federal law enforcement agencies and the Royal Canadian Mounted Police. In which agency, they wanted to know, did an officer expose himself to the greatest likelihood of getting hurt, or killed?

The answer was the United States Border Patrol.

Between 1919 and 1960, fifty-two inspectors were fatally shot, stabbed, run down by cars, or killed in air crashes while on duty. The majority met violent death in gun fights with smugglers or trespassing aliens.

The extra-high danger to life and limb in the Border Patrol is traceable to a tiny fraction of the thousands of aliens apprehended by the PIs. Ninety-nine of every hundred aliens are friendly, docile individuals. The violent fraction is the hard-core criminal element, the habitual delinquents—drug peddlers and smugglers, alien exploiters and other low types. Some of these loathsome criminals have been arrested as many as fifty different times; many have spent years in prison.

The following story is a good example of how such a hardened lawbreaker operates.

Inspector Earl F. Fleckinger was only 27 years old on that balmy day when he and PI Wilbur E. Kenny were patrolling the border near Calexico, California. Rolling down a country road, they came upon an ancient Model T Ford. What, they asked the driver, was he doing on this lonely stretch? The driver, whose name was Leon Rico, gave a vague and unsatisfactory answer. So the PIs searched his car and found many bottles of smuggled liquor.

They arrested Rico. Fleckinger, with Rico beside him in his government car, went ahead. Kenny, unarmed, followed in the alien's rickety Ford.

They had driven about a mile when Kenny saw the Patrol car swerve, then realized that Fleckinger and Rico were fighting in the front seat. Next he heard a shot. The Patrol car swerved off the road and smashed into a ditch.

As Kenny braked the Model T to a stop he saw Rico jump from Fleckinger's car waving a pistol. Shocked, Kenny realized the gun was Fleckinger's, snatched from the PI's holster by Rico.

The alien fired four shots at Kenny as the unarmed PI ran toward the Patrol Car. Then Kenny heard the hammer of Fleckinger's gun fall on an empty chamber. He tackled the alien, and the two fought viciously in the dust for several minutes. Kenny finally knocked Rico into unconsciousness and recovered his comrade's revolver.

He found Fleckinger lying across the front seat, unconscious. In vain he attempted to start the stalled Patrol car. He hailed a passing motorist, who rushed the injured PI to a Calexico hospital. There, that evening, he died.

THE BORDER PATROL PRODUCES CHAMPION MARKSMEN

The target range at the Port Isabel Academy permits as many as 50 trainees to receive firearms instruction at the same time. **(Left)** Students tally up their target scores. **(Right)** Experts give training in marksmanship with the pistol.

Kenny, believing Rico to be dead, rushed to Cal-exico to report the incident and to receive first-aid. Four other PIs hurried to the site to find that Rico had recovered consciousness and staggered across the line into Mexico, some 150 feet away.

United States authorities asked Mexican officials to turn Rico over to a United States court for trial. But, even though they admitted he had shot Fleck-inger, they refused to surrender him. Rico is prob-ably still at large today in Mexico.

From sad experience an unforgettable slogan has been branded into the memories of all Border Patrol-men: *Search all prisoners.* Those who forget it do so at their own peril.

PIs Anthony Oneto and John Fouquette were checking traffic on Highway 99 south of Indio, Cali-fornia. A car approached their station and, some distance before reaching it, slowed down. This is usually a signal that the driver would like to avoid questioning. PIs are always prepared to pursue such cars should the driver turn tail and run.

This driver, however, changed his mind and drew abreast of the inspectors. The driver and one passen-ger were in the front seat, and there were three men in the rear. Oneto questioned the four passengers and found them to be undocumented aliens.

Transferred to a Border Patrol car, the aliens told the inspectors they had been picked up by the driver in Mexicali, Mexico. He had made a deal with them, they admitted, to deliver them to Fresno, California, for seventy-five dollars apiece. They hoped to find jobs there in the fields.

Plainly the driver, Carlos Ochoa Romero—was a smuggler. Ochoa shrugged his shoulders and lied. He had picked up the men, he said glibly, only a few miles back. They were hitchhiking, he claimed.

Ochoa was ordered to drive ahead of the Patrol car into Indio. En route, Ochoa stopped his car several times. "Engine trouble," he explained. Finally he stopped, got out of his car, and walked back to the Patrol vehicle containing the two Inspectors and the four aliens. As he walked, he shouted he was out of gas.

Fouquette, driving, ordered Ochoa back into his car. He said he would push Ochoa's "stalled" automobile into Indio.

By this time Ochoa was alongside the Patrol car. He stooped, as if to say something to Fouquette, then shoved a gun through the window.

"Duck, Tony!" Fouquette shouted. They were the

last words Oneto was to hear on this earth.

Twice, Ochoa's gun blasted. The first shot killed Oneto, the second wounded Fouquette. Ochoa turned and fled.

Fouquette jumped from the car, pulled his sidearm, and fired. Ochoa faltered, but moved forward in a run. Fouquette pursued him for a short distance before his wound forced him to stop.

The four aliens, taking advantage of the confusion, jumped from the Patrol car in which Oneto lay dead, and escaped. Fouquette radioed Indio, and roadblocks were thrown across all arteries in the area.

The next morning, at 2:00 A.M., Ochoa surrendered to a highway check-point crew on Highway 99. He confessed to the shooting. Officers found the murder weapon hidden behind the dashboard of his car.

The four fugitive aliens were recaptured soon thereafter. The smuggler-killer was convicted of murder and executed in San Quentin prison.

Uncounted Border Patrol Inspectors have been injured, many of them seriously, in hand-to-hand battles with aliens. Among them were two PIs who arrested an invader in the El Paso city dump.

The Mexican, wearing spiked shoes, lashed out and raked the leg of one officer, opening a gash from knee to ankle. Then the wiry little man—he weighed only 127 pounds—jumped the second officer and injured him. As the PIs wrestled the alien to their jeep, the prisoner yelled for help from other Mexicans rummaging in the dump. The officers, still holding their screaming captive, were forced to take refuge temporarily behind the jeep. Stones, thrown by the would-be rescuers, rained down on their vehicle.

Chief Patrol Inspector Bill Davis, a veteran officer, painfully remembers the time he jumped a smuggler in the Rio Grande River.

"We just sank to the bottom and wrestled there for a while in the mud," he recalled. "It was simply a matter of whose wind gave out first."

Nor are smugglers and criminals the only hazards. PI Chet Wilson, on duty in the Yuma sector, will not soon forget the night he flipped on his flashlight while chasing an alien. As he pressed the button, the beam shone directly into the cold, beady eyes of a rattler coiled at his feet.

Instinctively, Wilson drew his revolver and fired—six shots!

"I didn't realize it until later," he recalled, "but I danged near shot off my own foot!"

Of course, he pulverized the sidewinder. PI Wilson has reported killing as many as twelve rattlers in a single day's duty, down in that desert country.

Others have had close calls with these death dealers. George Harrison, an old-timer in the Patrol, once was bitten on the hand by a cottonmouth. But PIs are made of stern stuff. Harrison recovered.

16
HOW ONE PLUS ONE
EQUALED FIFTY-NINE

Though an alien may attempt to cross at nearly any point along the 2,013 miles of United States-Mexican frontier, the Border Patrol knows from long experience that crossings are concentrated in certain favored areas.

At some points in the desert regions, well-worn trails still are visible. These were cut in the days before Operation Wetback, but are used relatively little now. In the mountains north of Yuma, one trail was cut to a depth of six inches by the endless parade of north-bound feet.

Today the Patrol keeps the situation fairly well in hand by concentrating its vigilance and strength on several key areas. Among these are the gateway cities themselves, and the stretches east and west of the entry gates.

Among the devices developed by the Patrol for entry-gate control are the lookout towers, looming high above the city and commanding a sweeping view of the line for miles in either direction. Three of these command the border at Calexico, California. Others overlook the line at Nogales, Arizona, El Paso and Laredo, Texas. These crow's-nests are manned continuously by inspectors, who are linked to their buddies on the ground by two-way radio. Observing an alien jumping the line, the tower duty officer relays the information to the ground. A patrol car or jeep in the area receives the tip, and immediately deploys to intercept the invader.

So that I could see how the lookout towers work, I was invited to climb to the top of one at Calexico. Standing at the base of the long, metal ladder, I wondered if I would ever be able to hold out until I reached the top. But under the gentle prodding of the Chief Patrol Inspector, I took a deep breath, grasped the first rung, and began the ascent.

After I had puffed and huffed my way up at least ninety rungs, I saw spread out before me—all of Calexico, all of Mexicali, and five miles of twelve-foot, chain-link fence, stretching horizon-ward from the crossing gate.

The twelve-foot fences have proved useful in discouraging border jumpers at San Ysidro, Calexico, El Paso, San Luis and other points where populated centers exist on the Mexican side. But the fences would prove meaningless without the Patrol to back them up.

Crews are constantly busy, repairing great holes chopped in the fence by would-be invaders with powerful wire cutters. On one occasion, in Nogales, Arizona, several holes had been opened. Spare sections of fence to close these breaches were not immediately available, and aliens were pouring through.

One ingenious officer devised a shrewd plan for catching the invaders. He obtained several cans of paint, each of a different color, and continually daubed the ragged wires which formed the margins of the holes. Each hole was given a distinctive color.

The officer then roamed the main streets and by-ways of Nogales. As dozens of Mexican citizens with

proper documents are always afoot in the streets of Nogales, it would have proved impossible to stop all Mexicans for questioning. So the PI merely looked for paint stains.

Spotting a "marked" man, the PI would approach him and ask:

"Let me see your documents, please."

"Me an American citizen," was a likely response.

"That's your story," the PI would reply. "But this red paint on your shirt tells another story. You just crawled through the fence."

The inspector would then proceed to tell the alien exactly *where* he crawled through, and approximately when. This clever scheme never failed to bring forth an ashamed confession.

Years ago a resourceful inspector hatched an idea for detecting illegal crossings which resulted in what PIs today call a "drag strip." These strips are created along the line in areas where crossings are known to be favored, and where the terrain permits.

To make a drag strip, officers in jeeps drag behind them a large timber, or a long section of chain, leaving behind a wide, smooth trail or strip. Such strips may be as wide as a city street, and some extend for miles. Prints left on the strips are spotted im-

A Border Patrol jeep is at work smoothing out a "drag strip."

mediately by officers patrolling in jeeps or by inspector pilots flying air reconnaissance over them. The strips are smoothed out regularly.

One enterprising alien tried to avoid the strip by pole-vaulting over it. Another crossed on stilts. Both were apprehended.

A Patrol pilot, flying over one strip, saw what appeared to be an animal's prints in the smooth dust. Then he noted that a man's footprints led to one edge of the strip where the "animal" tracks began. The human tracks resumed on the other edge of the strip, where the "animal" marks ended. This particular border jumper had walked across the strip backwards, on his toes like a ballerina, to create an unusual effect.

Though the great illegal migrations of the war years are now a thing of the past, thanks to tightened Patrol vigilance, some aliens still slip through the cordon. Of these, a few never reach their destinations. Now and then, PIs find a body in the desert, a victim of heat, thirst, starvation.

Most illegal crossings are made by lone individuals, or by pairs traveling the whole route together. But sometimes a "small army" will make the transit at once. The arrest of such an army is chronicled in

Border Patrol history as one of the Patrol's most remarkable captures.

Two PIs were standing line watch one dark night in Texas. Suddenly they heard several aliens approaching their stake-out point. They could not tell how many were in the approaching group, but the closer the aliens drew the more of them there seemed to be.

Because there were only two inspectors against an undetermined number of aliens, the two PIs agreed upon a daring plan. The first PI would fall in behind the leading alien, walking along behind him just as if he were a member of the group. The second inspector would wait until the last of the string had passed his hiding place. Then he would fall in behind the anchor man and shout the command: "Alto [Halt]!"

The first alien passed, and the first PI slipped quietly from his hiding place to fall in line. The second PI watched, in growing amazement, as the parade passed.

Thirty, forty, fifty! When the fifty-ninth—and last—alien passed, the second inspector left his hiding place, dropped in behind the anchor man, and yelled, "Alto!" His cry was instantly echoed by the first PI, who was already far ahead. The line stopped, dead still, in the desert darkness.

But now that they had halted the long parade, what would the two PIs do with all their captives? Again the PIs exercised rare judgment. First one inspector went off into the surrounding sagebrush, lit a match, muttered a bit to himself, snapped a few twigs; then his companion did the same. By repeating this maneuver several times, they gave the impression that the long line of aliens was surrounded. The Mexicans didn't dare to budge.

Then the PI in the rear slipped off very quietly to the Patrol car parked several hundred yards away. He alerted headquarters, which immediately dispatched a force to the site.

And thus ended the remarkable capture of fifty-nine aliens in one haul—by two lone PIs.

17
"STRONG, COURAGEOUS MEN..."

Like the Federal Bureau of Investigation, the United States Secret Service, and the Forest Rangers, the Border Patrol is today known and respected by citizens in all walks of life, from coast to coast.

The men of the Patrol, bronzed and weather-beaten men of action, command respect among their fellow Americans wherever they are stationed. Faithful to their tradition, they are ever ready and available for any task to which they are assigned, eager to serve their community and their country to the limit of their ability.

One newspaper editor, praising the spirit of dedication which marks the men of the Border Patrol, commented editorially:

"The people of this entire section appreciate very much the wonderful assistance rendered by the United States Border Patrol immediately after the disastrous hurricane of September 4. For several days, Border Patrolmen worked day and night, carrying wounded to the hospitals, helping to guard against looting and assisting us in many other ways during this troublesome period.

"It took strong, courageous men to work efficiently under the difficulties, and the well-trained, courteous Border Patrolmen did themselves proud. It took plenty of nerve to patrol the streets in the face of 100-mile hurricane winds with the air full of flying glass and timbers. No doubt some of these men had to leave their own families unprotected.

"We watched their cars go by all night long and it was a comfort to know that, if our house should go down, it would not be long before we would receive aid."

Key words, these—"strong, courageous men . . ."

It is difficult to describe and to measure the intense

(Above) A Senior Patrol Inspector at base station directs the operations of his mobile radio-equipped patrol cars. (Below) A typical Border Patrol Station.

loyalty of these men, both to one another and to their organization and work. It is this loyalty which unifies the Border Patrol. Those who really give their best to their jobs do so with fierce devotion.

I rode out of Yuma one day with one of the men on line patrol. Skirting the border, we jogged along in our jeep, hub deep in Arizona dust. As we talked, we passed through fields of maize and millet, castor beans and cotton. It was ninety-eight degrees in the shade, but my companion didn't seem to mind. In fact he appeared to thrive on the rugged working conditions which would have discouraged many a lesser man.

He talked freely and proudly, in his soft-spoken drawl, about his work. It was clear that to him the United States Border Patrol was the best organization in the world.

"If a millionaire was to come along and offer to set me up in any job I'd choose, with good pay for life," he said with conviction, "I'd ask him for the job I'm doing now."

APPENDIX

United States Border Patrol Sector Headquarters and Stations are located as follows:

SECTOR NO. 1. Houlton, Maine
  Stations: Calais, Maine; Fort Fairfield, Maine; Houlton, Maine; Jackman, Maine; Lincoln, Maine, and Van Buren, Maine.

SECTOR NO. 2. St. Albans, Vt.
  Stations: Beecher Falls, Vt.; Newport, Vt.; Richford, Vt.; Rouses Point, N. Y.; Swanton, Vt., and Whitehall, N. Y.

SECTOR NO. 3. Ogdensburg, N. Y.
  Stations: Malone, N. Y.; Massena, N. Y.; Ogdensburg, N. Y., and Watertown, N. Y.

SECTOR NO. 4. Buffalo, N. Y.
  Stations: Buffalo, N.Y.; Niagara Falls, N.Y.

SECTOR NO. 5. Detroit, Mich.
Stations: Detroit, Mich.; Port Huron, Mich.; Sault Ste. Marie, Mich., and Trenton, Mich.

SECTOR NO. 6. Grand Forks, N. Dak.
Stations: Bottineau, N. Dak.; Grand Forks, N. Dak.; Grand Marais, Minn.; International Falls, Minn.; Minot, N. Dak.; Pembina, N. Dak.; Portal, N. Dak., and Warroad, Minn.

SECTOR NO. 7. Havre, Mont.
Stations: Browning, Mont.; Havre, Mont.; Malta, Mont.; Shelby, Mont.; Sweetgrass, Mont., and Wolf Point, Mont.

SECTOR NO. 8. Spokane, Wash.
Stations: Bonners Ferry, Idaho; Kettle Falls, Wash.; Oroville, Wash.; Spokane, Wash., and White Fish, Mont.

SECTOR NO. 9. Blaine, Wash.
Stations: Bellingham, Wash.; Blaine, Wash.; Lynden, Wash., and Sumas, Wash.

SECTOR NO. 10. Livermore, Calif.
Stations: Fresno, Calif.; Livermore, Calif.; Sacramento, Calif.; Salinas, Calif., and Stockton, Calif.

SECTOR NO. 11. Chula Vista, Calif.
Stations: Campo, Calif.; Chula Vista, Calif.; El Cajon, Calif.; Oceanside, Calif.; Oxnard, Calif., and Temecula, Calif.

SECTOR NO. 12. El Centro, Calif.
Stations: Calexico, Calif.; El Centro, Calif., and Indio, Calif.

SECTOR NO. 13. Yuma, Ariz.
Stations: Blythe, Calif.; Wellton, Ariz., and Yuma, Ariz.

SECTOR NO. 14. Tucson, Ariz.
Stations: Casa Grande, Ariz.; Douglas, Ariz.; Gila Bend, Ariz.; Nogales, Ariz.; Phoenix, Ariz.; Tucson, Ariz., and Willcox, Ariz.

SECTOR NO. 15. El Paso, Tex.
Stations: Alamogordo, N. Mex.; Carlsbad, N. Mex.; Columbus, N. Mex.; El Paso, Tex.; Fabens, Tex.; Fort Hancock, Tex.; Las

Cruces, N. Mex.; Lordsburg, N. Mex.; Sierra Blanca, Tex., and Ysleta, Tex.

SECTOR NO. 16. Marfa, Tex.
Stations: Fort Stockton, Tex.; Lubbock, Tex.; Marfa, Tex.; Pecos, Tex.; Presidio, Tex., and Sanderson, Tex.

SECTOR NO. 17. Del Rio, Tex.
Stations: Brackettville, Tex.; Carrizo Springs, Tex.; Comstock, Tex.; Del Rio, Tex.; Eagle Pass, Tex.; Ozona, Tex.; Sonora, Tex., and Uvalde, Tex.

SECTOR NO. 18. Laredo, Tex.
Stations: Cotulla, Tex.; Hebbronville, Tex.; Laredo, Tex., and Zapata, Tex.

SECTOR NO. 19. McAllen, Tex.
Stations: Falfurrias, Tex.; McAllen, Tex.; Mercedes, Tex., and Rio Grande City, Tex.

SECTOR NO. 20. Port Isabel, Tex.
Stations: Corpus Christi, Tex.; Galveston, Tex.; Harlingen, Tex.; Kingsville, Tex., and Port Isabel, Tex.

SECTOR NO. 21. New Orleans, La.
Stations: Baton Rouge, La.; Gulfport, Miss.; Lake Charles, La.; Mobile, Ala.; New Orleans, La., and Pensacola, Fla.

SECTOR NO. 22. Miami, Fla.
Stations: Charleston, S. C.; Daytona Beach, Fla.; Ft. Lauderdale, Fla.; Fort Myers, Fla.; Fort Pierce, Fla.; Homestead, Fla.; Jacksonville, Fla.; Key West, Fla.; Marathon, Fla.; Miami, Fla.; Orlando, Fla.; Savannah, Ga.; Tallahassee, Fla.; Tampa, Fla., and West Palm Beach, Fla.

INDEX

ABOUT THE AUTHOR

CLEMENT DAVID HELLYER is especially qualified to write about the activities of the Border Patrol units on the United States-Mexican frontier. He has traveled by jeep, plane, patrol car and foot to explore this region in detail and talk with dozens of Patrol Inspectors.

Mr. Hellyer received his B.A. at The Principia College in Elsah, Illinois; his M.A. at Columbia University's School of Journalism; and has studied at the University of Florida's School of Inter-American Studies. As Latin American editor for the San Diego **Union**, he traveled extensively throughout Latin America and has, to date, lived in or visited all but two of the republics. Mr. Hellyer recently did research in Sao Paulo, Brazil, on a fellowship from the Pan American Foundation, and he is presently back in Brazil supervising the production of a travel guide on South America.

Co-author of **The American Air Navigator**, published in 1946, Mr. Hellyer has contributed articles to numerous newspapers and periodicals throughout the country—including **Life**, **The National Geographic Magazine**, **The Saturday Evening Post**, **Coronet**—and to several encyclopedias. He was born in Glendale, California, and he and his wife now make their home in Rio de Janeiro, Brazil, where his son shares his hobbies of fishing, stamp collecting, and underwater goggling.

U. S. LANDMARK BOOKS